Bullying in the Workplace, Home and School: Questions and Answers

Rev. Dr Tony Byrne,
Sr Kathleen Maguire
AND
Dr Brendan Byrne

BLACKHALL
Publishing

This book was typeset by Gilbert Gough Typesetting for
Blackhall Publishing
27 Carysfort Avenue
Blackrock
Co. Dublin
Ireland

e-mail: info@blackhallpublishing.com
www.blackhallpublishing.com

ISBN: 1 842180 68 1

A catalogue record for this book is available from the British
Library.

Printed in Ireland by
ColourBooks Ltd

Dedicated

to our three families

in recognition of their unstinting

love, concern and support.

CONTENTS

Acknowledgements

We give a special thanks to those men, women and children who have shared their experiences of bullying with us. Their honesty and courage have been an immense source of inspiration to us. We would like to thank all those who in one way or another have helped us to write this book. Ann Hanly, Lelia and Gerry O'Flaherty, Nuala Healy, Marie Murray, Claire Walsh and many other voluntary collaborators and colleagues were most generous in giving us their time and expertise.

INTRODUCTION

Bullying has always been with us, but there is clear evidence to establish that it is on the increase in homes, schools and the workplace. As a result of this increase, more and more people are asking searching questions about bullying. Why are people being bullied? What makes a person prone to be a bully? How does bullying affect victims? How can I prevent bullying? What practical steps can victims take to confront bullies? What effective strategies can be identified to address the problem of bullying?

In this book, we will attempt to answer questions that are often asked by participants at courses and seminars on bullying or by concerned parents and their children, who are victims of bullying both within and outside the school.

In Part I, Bullying in the Workplace, Dr Tony Byrne answers questions about workplace bullying. This section will help you to understand what workplace bullying is and will outline the more common forms of this kind of behaviour, offering some insight into why bullies bully. Dr Byrne analyses what the employer can do to prevent bullying in the workplace and how the law can be used to help victims.

In Part II, Bullying in the Home, Sr Kathleen Maguire responds to questions about bullying in the home. There is little scientific data on this type of bullying, partly because it is done behind closed doors and often people do not want to discuss it. This section analyses bullying from various perspectives and suggests ways to prevent it ruining home life and having a lasting, negative effect on children and adolescents.

In Part III, Bullying in the School, Dr Brendan Byrne

answers questions about bullying in schools. This section will help you to recognise bullying at school and to see what schools, teachers, parents and students can do to create an environment where bullying is not tolerated and where victims feel free to speak out against their aggressors. There will be a major emphasis on prevention.

The Appendix offers some reflections on bullying that can give affirmation, solace and healing to victims of bullying and those who care for them.

Lives can be shattered by bullying. To those who have experienced the devastation of bullying first hand, we hope to provide you with some comfort and encouragement. To those who have witnessed the bullying of an acquaintance, friend or family member, we hope to provide you with a wider understanding of bullying, how to recognise it and what to do about it.

Note

Every instance of bullying is unique in terms of how it affects its victims, the level of psychological pain it causes, the situation in which it occurs and the level of aggression of the bully. To deal with individual cases of bullying we recommend that the best course of action is to consult a professional in the field.

We hope this book will provide answers to some of the questions related to bullying in the workplace, home and school. However, we would like to emphasise that the *publisher, authors and their colleagues quoted in this book disclaim any liability* for any pain, injury, unpleasantness, stress or any other negative reactions or outcomes that may result from the use, proper or improper, of the information, suggestions or directives in this book. We do not guarantee that the information given herein is complete, nor should it be considered as a substitute for the reader's common sense or good judgement regarding job security, school regulations or the ethos of the home.

The information in this book must not be construed or interpreted to infringe on the rights of others or to violate the laws of the land.

Part I

BULLYING IN THE WORKPLACE

Rev. Dr Tony Byrne CSSp

Question   **How can I be sure that what I am experiencing is bullying?**

Answer   Many people who experience workplace bullying ask this question because deep within themselves they have doubts about their situation. They wonder if they are imagining what is happening to them or if they are exaggerating. Indeed, some asked, "Do you think I am going insane or becoming paranoid?" They move from a state of shock at being bullied to a state of denial. They say, "I know it happens to others, but I never thought it would happen to me". The feelings of shock and denial are often greater when it is a question of a man being bullied by a woman. Men are slow to admit that they are targets of female bullying. Those who are bullied often blame themselves and think they are at fault. "What did I do wrong? How did I set myself up for this situation? It is all my fault." The feeling of self-blame haunts them and causes added pain.

There is a certain sense of release when bullied people name the problem and are ready to say very frankly, "Yes, I am being bullied." The culture of silence is broken, doubts vanish and they begin to realise that bullying is the cause of all those sleepless nights, the pain in the pit of the stomach, the awful fear of facing yet another day at work and the haunting mental image of the bully.

It is helpful for those who are bullied to have a clear understanding of workplace bullying. The report of the Task Force on the Prevention of Workplace Bullying gives a concise definition:

Bullying is the repeated inappropriate behaviour, direct or indirect, whether verbal, physical or otherwise, conducted by one or more persons against another or others, at the place of work and/or in the course of employment, which could reasonably be regarded as undermining the individual's right to dignity at work.[1]

Question **Does workplace bullying have to happen in the actual workplace?**

Answer From a legal perspective in Ireland, workplace bullying can be carried out either in the actual workplace or in the course of employment. By law, it is not necessary that bullying behaviour be conducted by the employer or employees but simply by "persons". Therefore, the customers, business associates or independent contractors of the employer are all legally included in the definition of workplace bullying, so long as the bullying occurs in the workplace or in the course of employment, e.g. at training seminars, conferences or work-related social events.[2]

Bullying in the Workplace

Question   **Why am I being bullied at work? Why am I being picked on?**

Answer   Anyone can be bullied. It is not your fault; it is the fault of the bully. All types of people are bullied. People are bullied because they are good looking, not pretty, tall, short, stout, thin, they wear glasses, are clever, enthusiastic, competent, better qualified, pregnant, disabled, athletic, outspoken, efficient, popular, whistle-blowers, poor achievers, have high ethical standards, different sexual orientation, are single parents, divorced, married, recently bereaved, of different race and many more reasons.

My experience of assisting victims of bullies has convinced me that the majority of bullying situations centre on the fact that bullies feel inadequate and perceive the victim as someone who will expose their incompetence. Bullying in the workplace is usually psychological, stealthy and persistent. It involves many incidents, often quite small, but that, when monitored, show a clear pattern. The pattern will show that the bully is using bullying behaviour to subjugate, put down or eliminate the victims, or to make them feel upset, intimidated or afraid.[3]

Question   **What triggers bullying behaviour in the workplace?**

Answer   There are many factors that can trigger bullying. The most common of them are jealousy; popularity, trust and respect shown to the victim by other employees; the efficient and high level of performance by the victim; refusal to accept unethical or illegal instructions; challenges to the status quo; the victim is a whistle-blower; the victim is promoted or is made a trade union representative; the previous victim leaves; a new manager with a different management style is appointed. Bullying can also commence when there is a change of ownership or when new technology is introduced.[4] However, some characteristics of the victim may also trigger bullying behaviour, for example poor communications skills.

Question   **How common is workplace bullying?**

Answer   I was frequently asked this question during
                courses for trade union officials that I
                organised in Nigeria some years ago. The
                same question is often asked during the
                courses on Confronting Bullying. When
                victims are given information about the
                extent of workplace bullying it makes them
                realise that bullying in the workplace is a
                common phenomenon and that they are not
                the only ones who suffer in this way.

                Statistics from the European Foundation
                for the Improvement of Living and Working
                Conditions indicate that 9 per cent of
                employees in European countries have
                experienced workplace bullying.[5] The same
                organisation has stated that three million
                persons were subjected to sexual
                harassment, six million suffered physical
                violence and twelve million were subjected
                to psychological violence. It has been
                proven that strict anti-bullying policy is a
                deterrent to bullying. For example, Sweden,
                which has strict anti-bullying legislation, has
                an extremely low rate of bullying.

                The Economic and Social Research
                Institute of Ireland (2000) surveyed 1,000
                people in the workplace and found that 7
                per cent said they had been bullied in the
                six months preceding the survey. The Anti-
                Bullying Response Unit of the Health and
                Safety Authority of Ireland has stated that
                the number of requests for assistance they
                received from alleged victims has doubled
                in recent times.

Question   **What are the most common forms of bullying behaviour in the workplace?**

Answer   A wide variety of workplace bullying behaviour has been brought to my attention during the courses on Confronting Bullying and in telephone conversations with victims. There is physical bullying, for example pushing, shoving, kicking, hitting, poking, tripping, assaults, damage to property or interfering with one's work area. There is emotional bullying, for example threats, spreading of rumours and the exclusion or ignoring of victims. There can be non-verbal bullying also, when the bully makes suggestive, provocative and intimidating gestures. E-bullying is when employees send threatening or upsetting email messages or images. Mobile phones are also used by bullies to send disturbing messages. Damaging or interfering with the victim's personal property in the workplace can be most upsetting, for example damage to one's private car.

Victims often tell me how they suffer from constant criticism from the bully that is unjustified. The bullies make the victims feel they can do nothing right. No details are given by the bully as to what specifically is wrong with the victim's work and other colleagues see them as efficient and good at their job. Sometimes the victims' positions and status are removed in an underhand way. Their original tasks are removed from them and they are instructed by the bullies to do menial jobs or left without any work to do. The victims' desks are sometimes removed and placed in a remote area of the office where there is no phone. Access to resources and equipment necessary to do the work properly is denied to victims but is available to others in the workplace. Victims have told me that they have been isolated, snubbed or excluded from anything to do with the running of their department that was once part of their job.

Some bullies shout at their victims, especially in front of others. This is deliberately done to belittle, degrade and downgrade the victims. Victims are reprimanded for minor matters, while others who have made serious mistakes are not disciplined.

A common tactic of bullies is to avoid speaking directly to the victim. Essential information that may be needed for clarification is given by email or in short written memos. Totally unrealistic time-frames and deadlines are often given to victims.

One of the most painful ways of bullying is making jokes of a sexist, racist or ageist nature to torture the victim. The pain experienced in this way is added to by pestering, mocking, taunting, ridiculing, stalking or by attacking the victim's reputation by rumours, gossip or innuendo.

Unfortunately, bullies have been known to be involved in some appalling actions to torture their victims. These include ordering unwanted goods or services on behalf of the victims. A typical example is ordering a taxi at a very early hour of the morning. Bullies can encourage staff members to spy, snoop or eavesdrop on the victims. Mail can be interfered with, malicious letters sent to partners, friends and families as part of the extreme behaviour of some bullies. Some of the worst bullying behaviours on record include the bully sending a funeral director to the home of the victim or ordering books in the name of the victim on rats, unresolved crimes or other intimidating topics.[6] These kinds of extreme forms of bullying behaviour would seem to indicate that the bully is psychologically unbalanced and in need of in-depth psychiatric assistance.

Question   In my workplace, some employees try to brighten up the day with banter and fun, usually targeting one or two people in particular. Is this bullying?

Answer   Banter is a generally accepted part of the work environment and it can make the workplace more bearable if it is done in a light-hearted way without malicious intent. It can help a group of employees or managers to feel close and it can be a good way of reducing the monotony of the workplace. However, it would seem unfair that one or two employees should constantly be used as the butt of the banter and fun. My experience tells me that banter can get out of hand and can end up in a bullying situation. This happens when somebody is being constantly picked on about something that they find hurtful. If they show they are upset and feeling uncomfortable, the banter should stop. If it does not stop, then there is no doubt that what is going on is in fact bullying.

Even when no one person is intentionally targeted, there can be inherent danger in fun and banter. This is because what is defined as "fun" by one person can be absolute torture to another. People have all kinds of past experiences and sensitivities that can make what on the surface seems like a simple joke be a source of upset to a listener. The practical joke can be degrading and the innocent comment can be personal.[7]

Question   **Can I say I am being bullied if the perpetrator of the behaviour does not intend bullying me?**

Answer   Many victims of bullying blame themselves for what is happening to them. They say, "It is all my fault. This person who is causing me pain does not intend to bully me". Bullying is never the victim's fault; it is caused by the bully. It must be remembered that bullying by its nature involves persistent acts of aggression. It is difficult to believe that someone who persistently inflicts psychological pain on an innocent person does not intend to bully. Besides, the fact that a bully does not have the intention of bullying is not a defence in the courts.[8] What is important is the effect of the behaviour on the victim. If the action of the bully is unwelcome and offensive, humiliating or intimidating, then bullying is taking place, irrespective of the intention of the bully.

Question   **Are there common elements in bullying behaviour?**

Answer   Bullying is not a single act of aggression. There is always an element of persistent or continuous attack. The bullying behaviour is driven by a sense of vindictiveness, maliciousness, humiliation, cruelty, negativity, jealousy, intimidation and offensiveness. In many cases of bullying, secretiveness and irrationality are present in the behaviour.

Bullying renders the workplace dysfunctional. It inhibits employees and prohibits them from giving their best and most productive efforts in the workplace. Bullying behaviour has a negative effect on initiative, creativity, morale and job satisfaction of victims. It erodes a person's sense of self and makes the victim have self-doubt and self-blame. It has been known to cause 70 per cent of victims to leave their jobs.[9]

Question   I am bullied in the workplace and people call me a victim of bullying. I am not sure I like that label. Is "victim" an appropriate term?

Answer   Human language is limited. It can help us to be liberated and emancipated or it can oppress and put us down. The language we use labels the world we live in, both its limits and horizons. Should we use the term "victim"? This debate is not about semantics; there are deeper concerns here. If the term "victim" connotes or suggests helplessness, hopelessness or an inability to address the problem of bullying, then the term is not appropriate. However, if the term connotes deep psychological pain suffered by an innocent person as a result of bullying, or the destruction of the God-given dignity of a human person, then the term "victim" is indeed appropriate. That is why I have chosen to use the term "victim" in this book.

Question   Do you think that some employees try to escape from their responsibilities by crying "bullying"? Are some people using the problem of bullying to gain victim status? Are people jumping on the bullying bandwagon for their own selfish reasons?

Answer   Statistics on workplace bullying should leave no doubt that bullying in the workplace is a serious problem. However, it has to be said that there seems to be a tendency on the part of *some* people to escape their responsibilities in the workplace by claiming that they are being bullied. It must be clearly understood that fair criticism of employees' performance at work cannot be classified as bullying.[10] When extra work has to be negotiated to make the organisation viable, it is incorrect to call that bullying. The occasional difference of opinion or isolated expression of stress should not be labelled bullying.

We live in a society where it is commonplace to blame others for our own shortcomings. Responsibilities for the most hideous crimes can be transferred to others and not to the perpetrators of the crime. In this culture of blame, it is possible for perpetrators to claim that the effects of bullying behaviour were caused by other people and situations, and not by them.

Bullies, when challenged, often can refer to their own experience of being bullied and try to excuse their own bullying behaviour in that way. They should understand that two wrongs never make a right and that their bullying behaviour is totally unacceptable, despite their experience of being bullied.

In contemporary society, many employees stress their rights without any reference to their responsibilities. Where there is a right there is a responsibility to see that others enjoy their rights too. Employees and management must be conscious of mutuality in terms of rights and obligations. To emphasise one's rights at the expense of responsibilities can be a hidden form of bullying.[11]

Question   **What kind of a person is a bully? Are there some common characteristics?**

Answer   A bully is someone who coerces, persecutes or oppresses others through force or threats. Bullies have many common characteristics. They blame others for what goes wrong, never themselves. They are very insecure people who find it difficult to maintain healthy relationships with others. They have a tendency to become angry very easily. There is a strong desire in them to control others. They are extremely jealous and tend to take credit for other people's work.

However, there are two sides to bullies. They can be most charming to those they need to impress, especially people with authority. In my personal experience, my bully was so charming to others that few people would believe how I was suffering from the bullying experience. Bullies tend to twist the truth and are very devious. Their dishonesty can go so far as to accuse the victim of bullying.

One of the strong desires of bullies is to humiliate their victims. The wise words of the Talmud are relevant here: "You can kill a person only once, but when you humiliate a person, you kill that person many times over."

Question **Are there different types of workplace bullies?**

Answer Researchers have identified many types of workplace bullies. Marie Murray, who is a clinical psychologist and researcher, has identified the following types:[12]

- *The ideological bully*, who is driven by the misconception that employees will take unfair advantages if they are not coerced and bullied into working hard.

- *The reactive bully*, who has often had an experience of their kindness to others taken advantage of in the past and who is now determined not to be exploited again. The principle used by this type of bully is: do not give anyone an inch lest they take a mile.

- *The perverted bully*, who does not show concern or empathy towards others and who may disregard the pain and suffering inflicted on the victim.

- *The inadequate bully*, who has a great desire to feel important and who may need to oppress and control other people in order to feel powerful.

- *The defensive bully*, who fears their own lack of competence, ability, creativity and social skills. This kind of bully is envious and threatened by others who are talented in these ways.

- *The hierarchical bully*, who is being bullied from above by those with authority. Instead of tackling this problem and confronting the bullies above, the anger and frustration get displaced or passed down to those next in line. In this way, whole lines of people can bully those next in line to them, creating layers of misery in a workplace.

- *The immature bully*, who throws temper tantrums when challenged and when things do not go their way.

- *The insidious bully*, who quietly torments their victims through jibes, irritations, subtle changes in work allocation, providing misinformation, setting impossible deadlines, generating work overload or removing responsibility.

- *The isolating bully*, whose victims are cut off from clients and colleagues and who ensures that invitations to business meetings, social events, courses or seminars are no longer issued to the victim.

- *The defamatory bully*, who systematically erodes a person's good name through innuendo, body language, email, text messages, letters or gossip.

- *The paranoid bully*, who searches desks or personal belongings, eavesdrops on telephone conversations, interferes with letters or emails and maintains physical proximity.

These descriptions of types of bullies outlined by Marie Murray resonate with my own personal experience of being a victim of bullying in the workplace. My present contact with victims of bullying makes me believe that most bullies are a mixture of a few of the above categories.

Question   **I have considerable authority in the workplace and I am being bullied by some employees. Why are bullies often presumed to be people with authority?**

Answer   Research of bullying in the workplace in Ireland has established that 45.3 per cent are managers or supervisors and that 42.6 per cent of bullies are individual colleagues.[13] Anyone can be bullied – and that includes both managers and employees. It is wrong to think that bullying in the workplace is perpetrated only from the management to the employees. Bullying is pervasive in the workplace. Many managers are bullied by employees. Client bullying is becoming more common today, for example doctors and nurses being bullied by patients, teachers being bullied by schoolchildren and parents.

Question   **The woman who constantly bullies me acts in a most irrational way. She seems almost out of control at times. Could it be that she is mentally ill?**

Answer   It is understandable that you feel that way about your tormentor. From my experience of trying to help victims of bullying, I have learned that the vast majority of bullies act in a most cruel way. As I listen to stories of victims, I often ask myself what the mental condition must be of these aggressive bullies who will stop at nothing in order to destroy their victims, inflict the maximum psychological pain and yet never show any sense of guilt in so doing. Consultant psychiatrist Nuala Healy has stated in an interview that most researchers would say that bullies do not fulfil formal diagnostic criteria for anti-social personality disorder. However, they often display similar characteristics, such as pathological egocentricity, incapacity to love others, unreliability, untruthfulness, insincerity, lack of remorse or shame, a strong belief that people exist for them or an inability to accept criticism, challenge and blame.[14]

Question **Why is it presumed that men are not bullied?**

Answer Bullying is not a gender issue. However, male victims have told me that people are slow to believe that they are being bullied. It is presumed that men know how to protect themselves from bullies but the reality is that men are bullied as well as women. However, it must be understood that female victims far outnumber male victims. In a report of a survey of 5,252 employees made by the Economic and Social Research Institute of Ireland (2000), it is stated that twice as many females as males of 56 years of age or more were bullied.

Question   **My bully makes me feel like a fool. In fact, he says I am a fool in front of others. How can I deal with this problem?**

Answer   The bully may want to destroy your self-image, self-confidence and your whole sense of self. You need to be involved in activities, especially in activities that you feel confident doing. You need loving and caring friends with whom to discuss the problem.

When you are ready to confront the bully, tell them that you are not a fool and that you refuse to be treated like one. You may need to psych yourself up for this by practising what you are going to say and do over and over again, pretending that the "bully" is in front of you. Then, when you have rehearsed enough, you will probably feel more able to tackle the real bully. Make sure that other people hear what you say to the bully. Maintain your dignity and self-respect. Keep a detailed record of all the bullying incidents. Do not allow yourself to show your emotions before the bully by becoming tearful or looking frightened.

Remember that your bully is probably a coward who sees you as a threat and as someone who might expose them as incompetent. The bully probably dislikes you because you are popular, attractive and good at your job. You have a right to your God-given dignity. Do not let the bully take that away from you.

Question   There is a notorious bully in my work-place. Other employees have joined with him in bullying one of my colleagues. No one in the group seems to feel badly about this. The person who is bullied looks very sad and upset. Does this sort of behaviour happen in other work-places?

Answer   It is not uncommon for bullies to gather other employees to participate as collaborators in the bullying behaviour. Bullies are cowards and they need others to support them in destroying their victims. Bullies give favours to collaborators, ingratiate them, try to promote them and all this is done to make them depend on the bully. Bullies will try to turn the collaborators into "yes" men and women. This type of bullying is sometimes called "mobbing".

Bullies have low moral and ethical standards. When collaborators join in the bullying behaviour, the bullies somehow think that what they are doing is socially acceptable.

Collaborators usually get involved because they fear the bullies may pick on them if they do not co-operate. If the bullies are introverts, they will play a hidden role in the bullying behaviour and will motivate the collaborators to get involved by spreading untrue and nasty stories about the victims or by making the collaborators believe that bullying is good for the victims. If bullies are extroverts, they will lead the collaborators from the front and together with them will directly get involved in the behaviour.

All this causes unhealthy divisions in the

workplace. Those who co-operate with the bullies feel protected and untouchable, while the others feel marginalised. The favoured collaborators live in fear of falling out with the bullies and, in turn, becoming victims. They also fear that if the victims leave the workplace, the bullies will select another victim who might be one of them. It is easy to understand how this can lead to a work environment that is dominated by cliques, fear, unpleasantness, rivalry, factions, divisions and intrigue. All this creates negative effects on productivity, profit margins and customer services and increases absenteeism and stress.[15]

Question I feel most uncomfortable at work because of unwanted sexual advances by a bully. What can I do to resolve this problem?

Answer Some of the following insights on sexual bullying have been kindly shared with me during an interview with clinical psychologist Marie Murray. Sexual bullying is always very painful because it involves repeated, persistent, unwelcome and unwanted sexual advances that are upsetting and offensive. Sexual bullying takes on many forms in the workplace and the most common are "accidentally" brushing past the victim, sexually offensive conversations or remarks, displaying of pornographic materials, accusations of sexual promiscuity, name-calling with sexual connotations, making inappropriate or unsolicited acts of touching and jokes of a sexual nature.

The effects of sexual bullying are often deep rooted and varied. Some of these effects include a sense of helplessness, unhappiness, anger, depression, isolation, discomfort, entrapment, deterioration in relationships at work and at home, absenteeism, insomnia, general decline in both physical and psychological health, poor morale in the workplace, demotivation, apathy, poor team spirit and low levels of productivity. These negative effects are extremely painful for those victims who are not free to resign from their jobs because of family financial commitments, mortgages, repayments or the lack of suitable job opportunities. Sexual bullying can also have serious negative effects not only on victims, but also on other staff members because of the fear that they may be the next target.

A common misconception is that sexual bullying is suffered only by women. From my experience of assisting victims of sexual bullying, I understand that men are victims of sexual bullying by both women and other men. Female victims do not find it easy to admit that they are victims of sexual bullying but it is even more difficult for male victims because they may fear they will be ridiculed and will be regarded as weak for letting this happen to them. This results in a culture of silence and can cause very serious psychological problems.

In contemporary societies, many people are exposed to unwanted sexual abuse by unethical and explicit advertisements. In this type of obtrusive advertisement, men and women are presented in posters, newspapers, magazines, Internet and television advertisements as commodities to be used for sexual satisfaction. This type of advertising can be offensive, embarrassing and distressful to many people who are involuntarily exposed to it. It can legitimise, validate and promote sexual bullying in the workplace. Employers who fail to protect their employees from sexual bullying can be involved in costly lawsuits.[16]

Many bullies make offensive or nuisance phone calls. If this is happening to you, inform the police.

Victims of sexual bullying may find it difficult to confront their bullies because of the fear of reprisals or fear that people will say that the victims are responsible because they invited colleagues to have sex with them by dressing inappropriately. If fear inhibits victims from confronting the bully, it is very likely that the bullying will get worse and the victims may be totally devastated as a result.

You asked what could be done to resolve your problem. It is important that you consult your friends to determine that what is happening to you is truly sexual bullying. It is necessary that you keep a diary of all the instances of sexual bullying that you have suffered. Avoid all exaggerations in your record. Every detail should be noted, for example date, time, place, your reactions and the negative effects of the bullying behaviour. It would be advisable to list other people in the workplace who have been bullied, as well as the names of those who witnessed the bullying behaviour.

It may be helpful if you protest in a loud voice when the bully targets you. Make sure others hear you saying, "Stop. I do not like what you are doing".

It might be wise to ask the assistance of trusted colleagues. Ask them to observe the bully and to observe the bully behaving badly by visiting "accidentally" the place where they are operating.

To prevent or confront bullying, it would be helpful to check your body language (see page 40).

You may need to visit your family doctor and it might be wise for you to take some counselling.

Before making a formal complaint to your manager or to a board member, it would be wise to arrange a meeting with the bully and tell them that you will make a formal complaint if they do not stop the sexual or offensive behaviour, and if they continue to bully after that, you will not hesitate to take the matter further. Tell the bully that you have decided that you are ready now to solve the problem and that if they continue to bully you the consequences will be serious. This may frighten the bully and the bullying may stop, especially if you tell the bully you have made a diary of all the instances of bullying and that you have a list of witnesses.

If the bullying continues, then you should consider taking formal steps to stop the bullying. At this stage, it may be wise for you to take legal advice to assist you in making a formal complaint.

Question   I am receiving very upsetting email messages and it is causing me pain. Is this a form of bullying?

Answer   This type of bullying is called "flaming" and can be disturbing and hurtful. Email messages from bullies can be of a nasty or sexist nature. Pornographic material is sometimes sent to the victim by email. Negative memoranda are sent with the purpose of destroying the self-image of the victim.

How can a victim deal with "flaming"? The natural reaction is to get mad with the tormentor and return nasty email messages to them. That would not be the best action to take. It would be wiser to make hard copies of each offensive message and then show them to the appropriate people in the workplace. It is understandable that the offensive email messages can make the victim very upset and disturbed, but it is reassuring for the victims to know that this form of bullying is relatively easy to confront because evidence can be gathered against the bully. The source of nasty messages is easy to trace.[17]

Question   **Does the way people dress sometimes encourage people to bully them?**

Answer   In this imperfect world there is limited freedom as to what people can or cannot wear. We are all limited in what we want to wear because of the codes of dress enshrined in culture, age, climate, seasons, contemporary fashions and other factors. If employees are not sensitive to the written and unwritten codes, they may be vulnerable to the attacks of bullies in the workplace. Dressing too casually or too stylishly can trigger bullying. Bullies are always on the lookout for easy and effective ways of starting the bullying process. One of these ways is to use insulting and offensive remarks about one's dress.

Question I have been bullied at work for some time. I feel awful and I do not seem to enjoy life any more. Is this a common experience of those who are bullied?

Answer People who are bullied are often a little relieved to know that it is a common experience of victims to have health problems caused by bullying. The most common negative effects of bullying include loss of self-esteem and self-confidence that result in the following: feeling morose or sulky; tearfulness; experiencing a negative feeling about most things in life; long nights of sleeplessness; an inability to cope with problems leading to a sense of power-lessness; uncharacteristic outbursts of anger; feelings of worthlessness and frustration; mood swings; headaches; irritable bowel syndrome; bad or inter-mittently functioning memory; hyper-sensitivity; constant fatigue; and high levels of stress and anxiety.[18]

It must be emphasised that not all victims of bullying suffer from the physical and psychological negative effects mentioned above. Many who are bullied have strong inner resources that protect them from these effects. The support of loving, com-passionate and caring relatives and friends can prevent victims from experiencing many of the negative effects of bullying. However, it is important for victims who are feeling bad over a period to seek professional help from their doctors and to consider having the support of trained counsellors.

Question   **The man who bullies me is like a person who does not appear to have any sense of guilt about what he is doing to me. How can such a man live with the realisation that he is destroying me as a person and is inflicting tremendous psychological pain on me?**

Answer   Bullies never seem to feel bad about their unethical behaviour. My bully appeared to be at peace with herself. She was affable, jovial, polite and kind to other people, but to me she was cruel, offensive, aggressive and controlling. Bullies tend to be two-faced and deceptive. When I told people that she was bullying me, few would believe me. I felt that some people thought that I was full of self-pity and that I was exaggerating my account of being bullied. I wondered was I becoming paranoid. Many victims experience what I experienced and even worse. Some victims are told that they are jumping on the bandwagon to get compensation. The vast majority of victims do not confront bullies to claim compensation. Most victims simply want to have their dignity restored so that they can begin the process of healing and to enjoy life again. In her lecture on Confronting Bullying, Marie Murray has stated:

>   Clinical work with bullies shows that they often use unconscious psychological defences known as the defence mechanism. The bully may "rationalise" or justify their bullying behaviour on the grounds that otherwise the employees would abuse the system. Some bullies use "denial" and simply will not or cannot accept that their behaviour

is bullying behaviour. In some instances of bullying there may be "repression" which may take the form of conveniently forgetting the bullying outbursts or aggressive behaviour. There are people who divert their anxiety, anger, disappointment and distress into work achievements and this "sublimation" as it is called makes the bullies obsessed with controlling the work environment. A mechanism called "projection" can be used by bullies. When using this mechanism, the bullies attribute their own prejudices, envy, annoyance, suspicion or dislike to the victims. In this way, a bully who is jealous or threatened by the competence of the victim may accuse the victim of these emotions. Work with bullies has also shown that they may be competitive, driven, rigid and inflexible, easily aggrieved yet expecting other people to tolerate their irritability. They are also very angry when challenged and often believe that the best means of defence is attack. This is what makes working with bullies so difficult for other people in the workplace because when workmates complain the bully accuses them of having the problems the victims are complaining about.

Question   **The person who bullied me has been promoted and is highly appreciated by the board of management. Is this a common achievement by bullies?**

Answer   Bullies are often promoted in a workplace where there is no anti-bullying atmosphere and where organisations are insensitive to bullying. The bullies are promoted because it is said by management or board members that "they get the job done". However, this is a very shortsighted view and it is wrong to hold this opinion. Bullies destroy the initiative, creativity, morale and job satisfaction of employees and render the workplace dysfunctional. They inhibit and prohibit employees from giving of their best. They create a work environment where there is a high level of absenteeism, stress and loss of staff. They can involve their employees in costly claims for compensation. All these factors militate against the progress and development of the workplace in the long term.

Question   It is said that bullying is a learned behaviour. How do people learn to be bullies in the workplace? Does our modern society promote bullying?

Answer   Some people in this world have a deep-seated inner goodness and a sense of decency that prevent them from becoming bullies. Unfortunately, many other people, for a wide variety of reasons, become tormentors of innocent people and are engrossed in bullying behaviour in the workplace.

In our contemporary society, violence, aggression and bullying have become part of our entertainment world. Some computer games, films, songs, TV soaps and advertisements feed our minds with the erroneous principle that "might is right". Financial institutions and marketing promotions sometimes reflect the idea that profit is more important than are people. An example of this can be seen in the use of the "pester power" marketing strategy that aims to motivate children and teenagers to pester their parents to buy them expensive and unnecessary products. Society is dominated by aggressive, liberal and uncontrolled capitalism.

Workers and managers who are products of their society can bring to the workplace aggressive attitudes that can develop into bullying behaviour. It could be said that the increase in bullying is a symptom of a valueless, greedy and aggressive society. To tackle the issue of bullying it is necessary to address its root causes and create a more humane and people-oriented society.

Question **As a victim, what can I do to change or confront the bully who is making me so painfully miserable at work?**

Answer We must be aware that no one is totally bad in this world and no one is totally good. You, as a victim, who are suffering so much must avoid aggressive behaviour at all costs, even though it is understandable that at times you may feel like reacting negatively. You can be negative and hate the bullying behaviour, but do not hate the bully. Try to see the bully as a victim and as someone living in an unreal world, dominated, consumed and intoxicated by a desire for power over people, engulfed by negative emotions of hate, fear, insecurity, jealousy, unhappiness, low moral standards and a total absence of freedom to love. A person who takes away another person's dignity by bullying is a prisoner locked behind the bars of hatred, fear and jealousy.

Can you do something to change your bully? Perhaps, but the effort will sap up your energy and there may be no outcome. It is much easier for you to change and that can be done with a good deal of success. You can change some of your attitudes and your reactions to the bully and in so doing you might begin to change the bully even just a little. Perhaps you might like to consider the following plan of action:

Step 1: Diary

It is vital for you to keep a diary that records all the bullying incidents. Every little detail is important, for example the date, time, place, what was said or done, the tone of language used, the body language, the witnesses present, the effect it had on you and so on. Do not exaggerate the account; be as accurate and precise as possible. Bullying is not one incident, it is a collection of many bullying actions. When your diary is studied, a pattern will emerge and that will provide a clear understanding of what is going on.

Step 2: Building up your inner strength

As a victim, you may have lost some of your self-confidence and self-esteem. You probably had difficulty sleeping properly, and it is likely that you have not been feeling the best. You should not be surprised at these effects of bullying: they are often experienced by victims. Added to all these negative effects you may begin to think that it is all your fault and blame yourself. However, you must be convinced that the fault is with the bully, not with you.

You should visit your family doctor. It would be good to consider getting some professional assistance from a counsellor. Many victims tell me that counselling has helped them tremendously.

It is good to share your story with many caring relatives and friends. Talking is very therapeutic, as is crying. However, do not cry in front of the bully because that will be seen as weakness on your part.

Try to improve your social life. Have plenty of fun. Arrange to go to concerts, cinemas and other social events. Get more involved in activities you enjoy and are good at doing, for example golf, tennis, artwork etc.

You may be able to build up your inner strength by listening to soft music while reading some of the reflections you will find in the Appendix.

Step 3: Improving your body language

Research has consistently shown that in any oral communication, only part of the meaning comes across through the spoken word and the other part comes across through the speaker's body language, i.e. non-verbal communication. In preparation for confronting the bully, it may be useful for you to consider the following ideas that will help you to improve your body language.

Space

We are all territorial animals. We need to have our space respected. Your bully may want to invade your space as a way of irritating and intimidating you. There is a social space between you and other people. It is reserved for those who care for and love you. This reserved space consists of a distance of about 30 to 60 centimetres (1–2 feet) from you. Your bully should not be allowed to enter that space. The ideal space between you and the bully should be about 2 metres (6 feet). If the bully tries to get closer and enter the reserved space, you should simply step back or sideways. If the bully wants you in their office, make sure that you do not allow them to enter the reserved space. If they invite you to sit within the reserved space, simply move the chair, if possible, into the appropriate space.

Handshakes

Bullies and their collaborators may want to shake your hand as you enter a meeting or on some other occasions. In the past, our ancestors used handshakes to prove that they were unarmed and in peace. They tended to shake with their hands raised high. Bullies today sometimes use a special handshake that gives the message that they are controlling their victims. It is called the dominant handshake. This is done by extending the arm and holding the palm of the hand in a downward position even before contact is made by the other person. The bully begins to shake in a normal way and then when contact is made by the victim, they turn the victim's hand downwards while gazing at the victim in a downward direction. A good response to the dominant hand-shake is to put your right foot forward as you take the shake and try to bring the handshake into a horizontal position. The effect of this on the bully is that you are invading their reserved space and it gives the message that you know what is going on and you will not be put down by a dominant shake.

Keep cool

It is important that when you are in the presence of the bully, you keep cool. Do not get mad; get equal with the bully. Keep yourself under control. Speak slowly, clearly and deliberately but do not say too much.

Smile

Do not smile broadly. Try to smile with your

eyes, not with your whole face. The message you want to convey to the bully is, "You are not destroying me; I am taking you on very seriously and constructively".

Eye contact

Stare the bully in the eyes or just slightly above the eyes. Never drop your stare. This will get the message across to the bully that they have a tough victim to deal with. Remember bullies are cowards.

Dominant pose

The bully may try to intimidate you by folding their arms. Do not let that worry you. In fact, you might like to mirror the bully's tactic by folding your arms also. This will give the message to the bully that you understand what they are trying to do and that you are not intimidated.

Another tactic used by bullies is to hold their hands in a steepled upward position, something like the way people pray. This is done to convey the message that "I know it all. I will tell you what to do and you will listen to me". As the conversation goes on, perhaps you might like to hold your hands in a similar position and this will convey the message "I know it all too".[19]

Recommendations

The following recommendations may help you to improve your body language:

1. Do not walk fast or have jerky gestures in the workplace. Walking with firm steps will indicate that you are a strong person.

2. Stare the bully in the eyes or just above their eyes to show that you are not afraid of them.

3. Do not cover your mouth or eyes with your hand, to indicate that you are not intimidated by the bully.

4. Hold your head up high and keep your body in a straight, firm position to avoid giving the impression that you lack confidence.

5. Speak in a strong, clear, slow and determined voice to indicate that the bully does not frighten you.

6. Do not show any sign of fear in your facial expression. Do not have a pleading smile in front of the bully.

7. Do not wear clothing that makes you look inferior or superior to the other employees.

8. You should not nod in agreement to anything that the bully says to you at meetings, to indicate that you will not be bullied to agree with everything they say. Instead, say, "I'll think about it", "I'll talk with others about it" or "I'll get back to you about that matter".

9. Make good preparations for meetings with the bully. Try to anticipate what the bully will say at the meetings and what kind of tricks they may use. If possible, have a role-playing session with the help of your friends to rehearse how you will respond to the bully.

Step 4: Informal procedure

You as a victim may decide that you want to get on with your life and get on with your job. So you may choose to confront the bully in an informal and calm way rather than a legalistic, protracted and expensive formal way. To go the informal route, you should explain clearly to your bully that what they are doing is unwelcome and offensive and that it interferes with your work. If this is too difficult for you to do alone, then you should consider contacting other people – a trade union representative, a line manager, another employee, a human resource or personnel officer – and request confidentiality. You and the contact person should seek an interview with the bully and in a non-confrontational and calm way ask for a confidential interview to have the matter resolved. This informal route can show good results, though the bully may not respond in a positive way.

Step 5: Formal procedure

You may choose to go the legalistic, formal route or you may have tried the informal procedure without results. If that is the situation, then you may have to undertake the following actions:

• With the assistance of a professional legal adviser, you should present a formal complaint to your immediate superior or any member of the management.

• Your bully should be sent a copy of the formal complaint and told that a fair opportunity will be given for them to respond.

- The complaint should be examined by a designated and impartial member of the management. This is something to be arranged by the organisation or company for whom you work. Part of this examination should be to explore the possibility of engaging a professional mediator to look at the problem, provided the bully and victim agree to the mediation.

- If the examination as outlined above does not show a good outcome, then a formal investigation of the complaint should take place with a view to determining the facts and credibility of the allegations of bullying. Your legal adviser will instruct you as to what steps will have to be taken for the development of the proceedings.

The negative results of confronting the bully

It would be wrong to think that confronting a bully is an easy task. It is not easy. You must anticipate the bully's reaction. They will try to escalate the arguments to deny that they were involved in bullying behaviour. The bully may disclaim any knowledge of what you accuse them of doing and will argue that you are paranoid or that you are fantasising. However, your diary and hopefully your witnesses will counteract their false arguments.

The positive results of confronting the bully

As a result of your action in confronting the bully, you may frighten them to such a degree that the bullying behaviour may cease. The bully may see that you are approaching the problem in a professional and structured way and they may realise that the bullying must stop. As a result of your action, you may have saved your job. However, the most important benefit will be that you will have a great sense of liberation and freedom from the tormentor. All the efforts made to confront the bully are worth making.

Question   **Does bullying have any positive dimension?**

Answer   There can be some positive outcomes from bullying if the bully is confronted. The victim can experience a sense of achievement, liberation and satisfaction when the bully is challenged. The regaining of the victim's dignity and self-worth brings new life to the victim. If handled properly, confronting the bully can be a motivator for personal growth. The victims can discover through the process of confrontation a power within themselves for development. Their horizons can be broadened and they can discover personal qualities that can make them realise the richness of their own potential. One person attending the course on Confronting Bullying testified that because he confronted a workplace bully he realised that he had natural skills, qualities and abilities he never thought he had. He decided to organise his own business and his success has increased tremendously.

Another positive result of confronting bullies is that the former victim can be happy in realising that they may have saved other less gifted people from the horrors of bullying. This happens when bullies are reprimanded or dismissed from the workplace.

Many of those who have successfully confronted bullies reach out to other victims and try to help them. I know of a number of volunteers who are involved in this type of action. They advise victims and are available to them when they need to discuss their bullying experience.

Question   **Two people are being bullied in my workplace but they will not do anything about it. Why is this so?**

Answer   I can understand the reasons why those victims are slow to confront their bullies. In my own personal experience of being bullied, I was in a culture of silence and I believed that it was better for me to put up with the humiliation and psychological pain. I felt matters would get worse if I confronted my bully. In fact, when I kept quiet, matters got worse and the bullying behaviour became more aggressive and nasty. It took me a long time to realise what was going on and to name it as bullying.

    As I regained my psychological strength, I was able to challenge and confront the bully. However, in many cases, victims are afraid to challenge their bullies because they fear the consequences. They fear that they will not be believed, that they may lose their jobs or may not be promoted as a result of lodging a complaint. They may also fear that they will be refused a reference from their employer. In some cases, victims will not take action because they have known that others have complained and nothing was done about the bullying. However, a common reason for not opposing bullies is that victims have a deep-seated feeling that it is their fault. Bullies seem to be capable of sensing this feeling in the victim and they exploit it.

Question   My husband has been bullied very badly at work for the past six months. In recent weeks, he does not look himself. He has said he would like to die. I am very worried about him and I wonder is he suicidal. Can you advise me what to do?

Answer   It is wise for you to be concerned about your husband who is going through a tough time. He needs all the loving support he can get, but he also needs professional care. It is important for him to visit the family doctor as soon as possible and he should be encouraged to do this. He should also ask the doctor to arrange the appropriate professional assistance to deal with the problem. Your husband may need to see a psychiatrist, psychologist, therapist or a counsellor.

You must do all you can to give loving support to your husband. Try to hide your anxiety from him. If he sees you very worried and anxious, it may add to his tension and strain. Perhaps it would be good for you to know about the early warning signals or signs for suicide. I would suggest that you should look out for the following signs:

- unexpected and sudden change in behaviour at home, for example changing from jolly and bubbly to sad and morose;

- thinking and talking about death and suicide;

- showing signs of grief, stress and depression;

- becoming careless about personal hygiene and dress;

- getting involved in risky behaviour, for example walking on dangerous cliffs or swimming in very rough and dangerous seas;

- making jokes about suicide;

- religious despair – becoming suddenly negative about religious matters;

- making statements like "I would like to kill myself" or "life is not worth living";

- speaking about being reunited with deceased relatives or close friends;

- giving away treasured personal possessions;

- withdrawing from relationships at home; refusing to socialise with friends or staying alone in a room for long periods;

- playing music that extols suicide, or reading stories of suicide;

- revisiting places connected with memories of the past.

If your husband shows some of these behaviours, you should encourage him to talk about his feelings. It is important that your family doctor is kept informed about your husband's condition.

If your husband hints that he intends killing himself, praise him for having the courage to tell you. Avoid arguing with him. Do not make statements like, "It would be very cowardly of you to kill yourself", "You must not love me if you want to take your own life" or "You're only joking; you don't mean it". You must remember that your husband wants you to accept him as he is. He may be in such a psychological crisis that he is incapable of thinking the way you think. He may be totally engulfed in the most horrific flames of depression. The shutters of his mind may have closed. He may see no other way out of his awful pain except to kill himself. He may see suicide as the only way to get free of his tormentors, who are probably bullying him day in and day out at work.

If you see some of the early warning signals in your husband's behaviour, do not hesitate to act. Some people hesitate because they do not want to overreact but it is better to do something to help rather than not to act. Once you see the early warning signals in your husband's behaviour, you should go with him to the family doctor or, if he is in a critical state of psychological crisis, you should bring him to a hospital as soon as possible. Do not leave him alone. If possible, hide away anything he might use to kill himself, for example sharp knives, ropes, tablets and so on.

When the crisis appears to be over, If your husband has a sudden change in behaviour and seems to be recovering, you must be particularly attentive. People often kill themselves when the crisis appears to be over. They apologise to everyone whom they think they have offended and then they take their own lives. I would advise you to be extra attentive if your husband shows positive signs of recovery. At that time, your love and support, as well as professional assistance, may help him to survive.

Question My friend's husband was bullied very badly at work and as a result he killed himself. She is totally devastated by the sudden loss of her husband. What can I say to her?

Answer My sympathy and concern are with your friend because of the tragic death of her husband.

It is very difficult to pinpoint one single cause of suicide. Suicidologists believe that suicides are caused by cumulative burdens on the suicidal person. No one can be certain that the bullying experience caused the death by suicide of your friend's husband. However, researchers believe that 15 to 20 per cent of all suicides are caused by bullying.

Suicide is the most painful of all deaths for those left behind. It is estimated that more than 50 people suffer from blame, shame, loss, grief and rejection as a result of one single suicide. These people include relatives, friends, neighbours and colleagues. In virtually every circumstance, a person who has died by suicide was loved and was an important figure in a family and in a circle of friends did a great deal to enrich others. It would be a travesty if they were remembered and defined by their final act of desperation. Many people who have died of suicide have struggled a great deal. Very often it is unclear how long the struggle was going on. Research tells us that most people who died by suicide suffered from depression. For some, the struggle went on for years. For others, the struggle was somewhat short lived. Most of these people lived very productive lives and should be remembered as such. No person who died by suicide should be remembered as a failure, as a coward or as selfish. Suicide should not be described in those terms. Suicide is an act of complete desperation. Many people who have died by suicide have been engaged in great struggles to continue living and, finally, they ran out of energy, they ran out of hope. They were completely engulfed in despair and so they terminated their lives. It was not because they wanted to or because they did not love their dear ones or because they were weak or cowardly. They were people who had struggled long enough and succumbed to an illness – the illness of depression.

In the months and years following the suicide, often people who are left behind have gone through the initial stages of grieving and they are able to take a better look at their loved one's life. It takes time and effort to arrive at this point, but it will happen as long as survivors are patient and allow the grieving process to unfold. In this process, the survivors must struggle to rid themselves of blame, guilt and shame. They must realise that suicide is an act that is self-intentional, self-inflicted, leading to a cessation of life. The survivors cannot be responsible for an action of someone else that is self-intentional and self-inflicted.

It would be advisable for your friend to get some professional assistance from her doctor. She should consider getting some counselling and, if possible, attending a bereavement support group.

Question   **As an employer, what plans can I make to prevent bullying behaviour in my company?**

Answer   Prevention is better than cure. It would be wise for you to consult the employees' representatives and with them to identify a comprehensive, effective and accessible policy for addressing any future problems related to bullying and harassment that may arise. As an employer, you should declare in public that you want a work environment where a zero tolerance, anti-bullying policy prevails. Notices to that effect should be displayed in your workplace. It is important that you and the employees' representatives should design and implement a charter for appropriate behaviour that demands a high level of professional conduct and respect for the dignity of people in the workplace. The language used should be simple, direct and easy to understand. A copy of the policy and charter should be given to the employees and be available to new employees entering the workplace for the first time. A time-plan should be made for the evaluation and possible adjustment of the policy and charter.[20]

An effective strategy for the implementation of anti-bullying policies has been used by some companies in Ireland. In this strategy, the employees are asked by the management to elect a few employees to take on the role of anti-bullying contact people. A job description should be written for the contact people. The selection of contact people should take into account the various categories of employee, for example race, gender, age and so on. When elected, these contact people should be sponsored by the company to attend seminars and short-term courses on bullying. When they are trained, maybe they should be offered a small stipend over and above their normal wages. After a period of two years, the contact people should be evaluated by the employees.

Question   **What style or model of management prevents bullying in the workplace?**

Answer   Bullies can prevail in any workplace irrespective of the style of management. Bullying is secretive, stealthy, clandestine, covert and surreptitious. Managers may not be aware of what is going on and employees will not inform them because they fear the bully. If they expose the bullying that is going on, the consequences may be horrific for them. Therefore, it is important for management to be vigilant and watch out for bullies among the employees.

Researchers in Ireland and abroad are agreed in their belief that the old-fashioned boss–management style of administration promotes and feeds into a workplace environment where bullies can be accommodated. In this type of management, the presumption is that workers can be coerced into doing tasks by the promise of rewards or the threat of sanctions. This type of insensitive and inhuman management style downplays the importance of the psychological needs of the employees, especially those of job satisfaction and fulfilment. The "top-down" or "upstairs/downstairs" form of management can destroy creativity and can promote bullying. The boss–management style has been questioned and is now generally regarded as non-productive, outdated and non-viable for employees today. The leader–management is a more productive option because it seeks to achieve a happy, fulfilled, highly motivated workplace. In this model of management, there is respect for the God-given dignity of the human person and basic psychological needs are fulfilled. Employees feel valued, respected, cared for and are invited to participate in setting reasonable targets. Emphasis is on co-operation and not rivalry. Bullies find it difficult to operate in this type of work environment.

Question   **I am being bullied in my employment and I need to contact an organisation that could help me. Can you suggest some contact?**

Answer   There are many sources that can help you. The following is a short list of resources, but there are many others not included in this list.

• The Anti-Bullying Centre at Trinity College, Dublin, Tel: (01) 6082573, www.abc.tcd.ie. It provides a free information service, talking people through their options. Other services include counselling and psychological assessment for legal cases; independent investigations at the request of employers; and workshops.

• The Health and Safety Authority's Bullying Response Unit, Tel: (01) 6147000/ 6147139, www.has.ie, provides victims with informa-tion on their options.

• The Labour Relations Commission, Tel: (01) 6136666, www.lrc.ie, has dealt with a number of individual bullying grievances through mediation by the Advisory Development and Research Services. Rights Commissioners are independent adjudicators and they investigate disputes referred to them by individuals or small groups of workers under specific legislation.

• The Employment Rights Information Service, Tel: (01) 6313131, www.entemp.ie, provides information on employment law.

- The Equality Authority, Tel: (01) 4173333, www.equality.ie, investigates complaints of discrimination on specific grounds.

- CaB, The Campaign against Bullying, can be contacted at: 72 Lakelands Avenue, Stillorgan, Co. Dublin, Tel: (01) 2887976, Email: odonnllb@indigo.ie, www.Clubi.ie/killick/CaB/

- Delma Sweeney, Conflict Resolution and Mediation Consultant, 1 Olney Mews, Rathgar Avenue, Dublin 6, Tel: (01) 4966697, Email: delmas@eircom.net

Question   **Does mediation help to address the problem of bullying in the workplace?**

Answer   Mediation can have a variety of meanings. However, in terms of a bullying situation it should be understood as meaning a confidential process that enables people in a conflictual relationship to resolve their conflict in a mutually agreeable manner with the assistance of a trained mediator who is a neutral party. Professional mediators can be effective, especially if they have specialised in the problem of bullying and are experienced in their profession. Mediation is a problem-solving technique that helps disputing parties who are willing to participate in the process. It should be remembered that mediators do not solve the problems of the disputing parties. The main function of the mediator is to help the parties themselves to find solutions to the problem. Neutrality and the avoidance of blame are key factors in the mediation process.[21]

Question **Can the law of the land help me as a victim of workplace bullying?**

Answer Resort to legal action should be made only when everything else has been tried and has failed to help the victim. Engaging in legal proceedings has been found to be pro-tracted, expensive, complicated and does not always show good results. Besides, victims of bullying can be so mentally fragile as a result of their horrific experience that they may find court appearances too stressful. However, if the decision is made to proceed with litigation, it is advisable to engage solicitors or barristers who spe-cialise and are experienced in this area of bullying and stress at work.

Section 6 of the Safety, Health and Welfare at Work Act (1989) gives a good indication of how victims can benefit from legal action. It states:

> An employer has a duty of care to ensure the health, safety and welfare at work of all employees. Non-physical forms of bullying, violence or excessive levels of stress as suffered by employees may be proved unlawful and the employer is liable to pay compensation.

Barrister John Eardly, in *Bullying and Stress in the Workplace*, refers to the stress-related consequences of bullying and harassment that include depression, reduced self-esteem, phobias, sleep disturbances, post-traumatic disorders and so on. Eardly states that these consequences might persist for years after the incidents of bullying and harassment and can cause social isolation and family financial problems. As a result, the legal damages arising from bullying and harassment stress cases can be high.

Sweden has legislation dealing directly with bullying and the rate of workplace bullying in that country is the lowest among European countries. Unfortunately, bullying in the workplace is not addressed explicitly by law in Ireland and one would hope that this situation would be changed. However, the problem of bullying can be tackled at three levels: common law, discrimination legislation or by the Health, Safety and Welfare legislation.

Employers have, by law, a general duty of care towards their employees. A claim for personal injury based on an alleged negligence or breach of duty of care on the part of an employer must be brought within three years from the date of the cause of the injury or the date of the knowledge of the injury. Injury in this context includes any impairment of a person's physical or mental condition. In cases of severe bullying over a period of time, a victim may suffer mental impairment in terms of stress, anxiety or related problems.

It is worth noting that the Safety, Health and Welfare at Work Act (1989) Section 13, places a duty on employers to consult employees regarding measures to ensure safety, health and welfare at work and also to assess the effectiveness of such measures. Section 13(3) enables employees to appoint a "safety representative" to represent them with their employer. Safety representatives have extensive powers and rights, for example a right to investigate potential hazards and complaints made by an employee related to health, safety and welfare at work. If an employee is experiencing bullying behaviour, they may bring the matter to the safety representative, the management and/or the employer. If the matter is not addressed properly, the complaint can be brought to the attention of the Health and Safety Authority, which has the main enforcement function under the legislation. It is worth noting that failure to discharge the duties imposed by the 1989 Safety, Health and Welfare at Work Act is a serious offence.

A way of legally challenging bullying in the workplace is to use the Employment Equality Act of 1977. This Act prohibits discriminatory treatment in the workplace on grounds of sex or marital status. If an employee experiences this form of bullying, the first action should be to communicate to the perpetrator that the behaviour is offensive and unwanted. If the problem continues, a complaint should be brought to the attention of management, the employer and union representative. The Employment Equality Agency can give advice if requested. If the complaint is not resolved internally, the complainant may choose to follow the legal process provided for in the 1977 Act.

Endnotes

1. *Report of the Task Force on the Prevention of Workplace Bullying* (2001) Stationery Office.
2. John Eardly (2002) *Bullying and Stress in the Workplace*, Dublin: First Law Ltd, p. 187.
3. Tim Field (1996) *Bully in Sight*, Oxfordshire, UK: Success Unlimited, p. 95.
4. David Graves (2002) *Fighting Back*, London: McGraw-Hill Companies, p. 57.
5. Anti-Bullying Research and Resource Centre (1998) *Workplace Bullying: Key Facts*, Dublin: Educational Department, Trinty College, p. 4.
6. Tim Field (1996) *Bully in Sight,* pp. 41–6.
7. David Graves (2002) *Fighting Back*, pp. 35–6.
8. John Eardly (2002) *Bullying and Stress in the Workplace*, p. 12.
9. Jacinta M. Kitt (8 July 2003) "Bullying in the Workplace", RTE 1 radio broadcast.
10. David Graves (2002) *Fighting Back*, p. 3.
11. Tony Byrne, CSSp (1988) *Working for Justice and Peace*, Ndola, Zambia: Mission Press, p. 8.
12. Interview with clinical psychologist Marie Murray (30 August 2003).
13. *Report of the Task Force on the Prevention on Workplace Bullying* (2001) p. 41.
14. Consultation with consultant psychiatrist Dr Nuala Healy (19 August 2003).
15. Andrea Adams with Neil Crawford (2000) *Bullying at Work*, London: Virago Press, p. 13.
16. John Eardly (2002) *Bullying and Stress in the Workplace*, p. 121.
17. David Graves (2002) *Fighting Back*, p. 42.
18. Lucy Costigan (1998) *Bullying and Harassment in the Workplace*, Dublin: The Columba Press, p. 71.
19. Peter Clayton (2003) *Body Language at Work*, London: Octopus Publishing Group Ltd, p. 32–3.
20. Tony Byrne, CSSp (1992) *How to Evaluate*, Ndola, Zambia: Mission Press, Chapter 2.
21. Conflict Resolution and Mediation Consultants, Dublin: 1 Olney Mews, Rathgar Road.

Part II

BULLYING IN THE HOME

Sr Kathleen Maguire PBVM MA

Question   **I am not sure if the disturbing behaviour in my home is bullying. What is meant by bullying in the home?**

Answer   Generally, bullying in the home can be seen as any form of emotionally or psychologically negative action directed towards an individual or individuals. It must be remembered that bullying is not just a once-off incident between people. If there is behaviour in your home that is unprovoked, repeated, stressful and very hurtful, then you have a bullying situation.

Question   **What are the common forms of bullying in the home?**

Answer   There is little or no scientific data available to establish the extent and the various forms of bullying in the home. Part of the reason is that domestic bullying is done behind doors in secret where it is difficult to assess objectively what is going on and how the tormentors inflict psychological pain on victims. However, my pastoral experience of working with families over a very long period leaves no doubt in my mind that bullying in homes is a serious problem for many people and it takes on a wide variety of forms.

Another reason for the absence of information is that parents, partners and children tend to maintain silence about the problem to avoid either embarrassment or reprisals by bullies.

The presence of a bully destroys peace and harmony in the home, not only for the victim but also for all the members of the household. The effects can be widespread, for example children who observe bullying in the home tend to replicate it in adulthood.

Domestic bullying is essentially about control. That control can be related to people's minds, movements, finances, sexuality, dress, associations, beliefs, heating, food, hospitality, freedom of expression, academic development, personal relationships, feelings, emotions, recreation or expressions of individuality.

A key factor in domestic bullying is the urgent and persistent criticism of the victim who is made to believe that they never get it right and are totally incompetent and lacking in intelligence. Added to all this, there can be a total lack of appreciation by the bully for the contribution the victim is making to the home.

Those who suffer domestic bullying are slow to confront the bully because of a relationship of dependence between the bully and the victim. Domestic bullies use the element of dependence to suppress and destroy the God-given dignity of those in the household.

Question   **Is teasing a form of bullying in the home?**

Answer   Most families enjoy some harmless teasing.
We all like to "leg pull" from time to time.
We usually feel comfortable with our own
families so we take liberties with them that
we would not dare to take with others.
Playful teasing that does not hurt is fine.
However, there is a risk of carrying the joke
too far. A twelve-year-old girl from what I
believed to be a very happy family said to
me, "I hate home". Needless to say, I was
quite taken aback. When I succeeded in
getting her to share with me why she hated
home she burst into tears and said, "My
brother never stops teasing me and he
thinks it's funny". We must be very careful
how, when and whom we tease. People
react differently and we all have different
sensitivities.

Teasing can be regarded as a form of
verbal aggression and can make another
person feel self-conscious and excluded.
Generally, it makes people feel bad and in
this respect, there is a very thin line between
teasing and bullying.

Within the family, we must avoid all types
of teasing that ridicule or put someone down.
Teasing of a younger sibling by an older
brother or sister can be quite damaging. It
can be a form of bullying and we must be
very vigilant in knowing where to draw the
line, otherwise what appears to be innocent
teasing could develop into serious bullying
with painfully negative effects.

Question   Why do bullies bully? What drives a person to be involved in bullying behaviour? What are the root causes of bullying in the home?

Answer   Each bullying situation is different and bullies can operate with different mindsets. My experience of listening to accounts of how people are being bullied in their homes brings me to the conclusion that there is no one universal cause that makes one person bully another. However, many professionals would suggest that one of the root causes of bullying might be centred on attitudes acquired by bullies in their early years in the home and in families.

Some researchers believe that children who do not receive love and affection from their parents or who are criticised unduly may be prone to aggressive behaviour in later life. Another possible theory is that children who observe aggressive behaviour in their parents and other adults tend to identify with this behaviour and imitate it.

Other researchers tend to believe that bullying attitudes are acquired in children who are continuously controlled by parents. The children are not allowed to behave badly but their parents do not explain why they cannot act that way. A battle situation arises between the parents and the children. The children want to act in an inappropriate manner and they are told to "stop" but no reason is given to the children why they have to stop acting that way. A struggle ensues and the children lose the battle because of parent power. As the children develop into adolescence and adulthood, the memories of lost battles are deep-seated and there is a strong desire within them never to lose battles again. The result is that they tend to act badly when there is no parent to force them into submission.[1] This mentality is carried with them into adulthood. When they cannot act as they like and when they are opposed or challenged by others later on in life, they may tend to use every means possible, foul or fair, to avoid losing another battle, even if that means using extreme forms of bullying.

Question   **What triggers bullying in the home?**

Answer   It does not take too much for bullying to be triggered in a home. Neither does it take much for bullying to develop and make the home a most unpleasant place to live. Homes are places where people interact frequently and closely in a limited space. The more frequent and closer the interaction and the more limited the space the greater the possibility of bullying behaviour. People need private space and the opportunity to demonstrate their individuality and independence. If those important needs are not met in the home, then tension, frustration and irritability can be experienced. Bullying tactics can be used as a way of coping with these negative emotions.

Homes are places where we expect people to listen to our stories – not just words but also our feelings. If that does not happen, we can be so disappointed that we protest by using bullying tactics.

In my pastoral experience of helping people to improve the quality of their relationships in the home, I have found that unequal levels of education in homes can lead to bullying. Those with less education can feel threatened by those with more education. Those without academic qualifications can develop a poor self-image and be tempted to cope by bullying behaviour. I have noticed that in some homes people who are better informed because of their education can dominate those with lesser education.

It is often said that money is the root of all evil. Bullying can be triggered in homes where there is a lack of dialogue about monetary matters and where there is an absence of a democratic approach to family budgeting and the distribution of financial resources.

Setting boundaries for appropriate behaviour of teenagers and young adults in the home can trigger bullying. Bullying methods by the offspring or parents can be used when there is an absence of dialogue or when rules are imposed without negotiation.

Question **I am suffering greatly because I am being bullied by my husband in the presence of my child. I am wondering what effect this will have on my child.**

Answer Of course you are worried – and you have good reason to be concerned, because you have two problems to deal with: the effect the bullying has on you and on your child.

I suggest you first explore how you would deal with your own problem of being bullied by your husband. Perhaps you would consider the following points:

1. Start by making a list of all your good qualities. It is important to try to maintain your self-esteem during this difficult time.

2. Then try to list your husband's good qualities, remembering that he is not totally bad.

3. Observe your husband and list all the benefits that he gains through his bullying behaviour. See how many of these benefits he might gain by having a non bullying manner.

4. Take a good look at yourself and see if there are changes you could make in your behaviour that would help the situation.

5. Become aware of your own feelings of anger and annoyance, and avoid bullying tactics. Then do something about these feelings: for example, give yourself time to be alone in a quiet place, relax, listen to soft music, pray,

light a candle or use any other means to help you to relax (see Appendix).

6. Try to discover if something triggers the bully's anger or frustration.

7. Take a course in self-assertiveness. This may help you face the situation in a structured and effective way.

8. Be realistic about your efforts and do not expect perfect results.

9. Consult your family doctor to make sure you are in good health because the process of solving problems carries with it stress and strain.

Now let us reflect on how the bullying situation in your home can affect your child. A child is particularly vulnerable to bullying at home. The abuse of power is one of the saddest betrayals of trust. Bullying has a detrimental effect on the child in the home. However, the extent of the harm done will depend on a number of factors, including:

• the level of seriousness of the bullying;

• how old the child was when the bullying started;

• what quality of support was available to the child at the time of the bullying.

If at the time of the bullying there were other people available to comfort, console and reassure the child, then the harm done may have been lessened by the care, support, affirmation and kindness that the child received.

The following are some of the effects of domestic bullying on a child:

- showing extremes of behaviour, such as being excessively restless and demanding, looking for attention or being timid and withdrawn;[2]

- looking sad, upset and tearful;

- being withdrawn from adults or showing nervousness in the presence of adults;

- showing an inability to talk about the ordinary events of the day;

- complaining of physical illness, such as stomach-aches, headaches, dizziness and tiredness;

- constant bed wetting, for which there is no medical cause;

- adopting rigid or defensive body postures;

- showing a lack of concentration and poor school performance;

- bullying those who are younger and weaker.

I would suggest that you observe your child carefully to see if they show any of these symptoms.

Question   **My son of seven years old is bullying my five-year-old daughter at home. As a parent, what should I do to encourage him to stop?**

Answer   To encourage your son to stop bullying, I would suggest that you consider some of the following suggestions:

- *You must act quickly!* When your son bullies he is in a heightened emotional state and it may be difficult to stop this emotional behaviour. It is, however, essential that you do so, particularly if his little sister is in danger of being hurt.

- *Separate the bully from the victim.* If you happen to witness your son bullying, separate him immediately from your daughter. Explain to him that the behaviour you have witnessed is very wrong.

- *Listen to both sides.* If you have witnessed what happened, try to calm down your son and others in the home who may be upset. Listen to both sides in order to determine exactly what happened.

- *Dialogue with your son.* Most children need a cooling off time, even a few minutes help. Stand or sit with your son. Let him see that he is responsible for his aggressive actions. Try to get him to accept this.

- *Help your son to identify the cause of his bullying.* You may have to ask him questions like, "I think you pushed your sister because you wanted to take her jigsaw. Is that right? Wasn't there another way to get the jigsaw? Did you try asking her for a loan of it?" Your son needs help in understanding his behaviour.

• *Help your son to accept distress.* Explain to your son that everyone gets upset sometimes and that there are easier and better ways to solve problems. Tell him that people cannot always get what they want.

• *Tell your son that he must apologise.* Calmly explain to him the importance of apologising for the wrong he has done. If he is reluctant to do so, wait until he has calmed down and is less angry.

• *Overcome embarrassment.* If your son by his bad behaviour embarrasses you in public, just address the issue with him so that he does not think it is okay to do mean things in a situation where he thinks he will get away with it. You may feel embarrassed and want to cover up his behaviour but it is much better to correct him quietly on the spot. He will learn not to take mean advantage over you. Do not worry about other parents who may be looking on; they will understand all too well.

• *Reward good behaviour.* You must always acknowledge and reward the good behaviour of your son, whether it is a room well tidied, a game well played or an honest effort to improve behaviour at home.

• *Get help if needed.* If your son continues to bully and if his aggressive behaviour gets worse, it may be necessary for you to ask advice from a doctor or child psychiatrist.

- *Learning to ask permission.* Young children need to learn to ask permission and not to act independently of their parents. This helps them to be disciplined and can prevent them from using bullying tactics to get what they want.

- *Boundaries.* Parents must be in total agreement about the boundaries they set for their children's conduct in the home. If they allow their children to trespass these boundaries because of the pressure put on them by the children, they may be giving the message that bullying is a way to get what they want.

- *Gently discipline your child.* Your son who bullies needs to experience gentleness and discipline. For example, if you observe him being aggressive at play take him out of the game for a few minutes, telling him, "You may go back and play with your friends when you play fairly. If you want to continue to play roughly, you will have to stay out of the game today and play another time." Over a period, your son will begin to learn that bad behaviour is unacceptable to you and that it deprives him of good fun.[3]

Question **How does bullying in the home affect adolescents?**

Answer Adolescent years are very special. Adolescents, though not normally aware of it, are struggling to break away from childhood and grasp onto the desired mature adulthood. It is a beautifully enriching and challenging time; it is a time of new creations, ambitions, explorations and adventures. It is also a time of great confusion and pain. During these very vulnerable and formative years, adolescents develop through many different stages. So life, though full of excitement, is also filled with great challenge, struggle and the pain of coping with change.

For adolescents, bullying in the home intensifies the pain and confusion of this very sensitive time in their lives. They find it difficult to find words to express their negative emotions. However, their body language can give us some clues of the serious negative effects of bullying in the home. Their eating habits may change and they may eat either too little or too much. They may refuse to join their friends for social evenings, not return phone calls or emails, lose interest in sporting activities, give abrupt responses to questions, look unhappy and aggressive, become dis-interested in studies, absent themselves from school, gaze at television for long hours without concentrating on what is shown, play music loudly at inappropriate times, suffer from insomnia and stomach pains and, in some instances, they may increase their alcohol and drug intake. When bullying intensifies at home, the adolescent may run away, sometimes doing so with an older person whom they have contacted on the Internet. This type of reaction is becoming more common and is causing parents and the police much concern.

Adolescents can feel extremely guilty when they observe their parents or others being bullied at home and cannot do anything to defend them or to stop the bullying behaviour. In some extreme situations of domestic bullying, adolescents consider the option of suicide. They usually do not tell parents about their suicidal intentions but sometimes they tell their peers.[4]

Question **What advice would you give to us as parents to help our twelve-year-old daughter who is being bullied by her fifteen-year-old brother?**

Answer To address this problem it will be necessary for you to give attention to your daughter who is the victim of bullying by her brother. You also have to attend to your fifteen-year-old son who is the bully.

Let us first consider what steps can be taken to help your daughter.

- *Reassure her.* The first and most important thing you need to do is to reassure your daughter of your love and support. Make it clear to her that you are aware of her brother's behaviour and of her deep pain. Assure her that you are there to protect her and care for her.

- *Be vigilant.* You must be very vigilant because of the possibility of depression. This may include changes in behaviour in relation to eating habits, sleep and school performance.

- *Get help.* If your daughter continuos to be upset, you should consult your family doctor and ask that she be referred to the appropriate service, for example the child guidance clinic. Consult your doctor also on the possible need for family therapy, which can be arranged for you if necessary by the family doctor.

- *Work together.* It is important that both parents work together in this situation. This may not be possible in cases of marriage separation or single parenting but, in the interest of the child, such mutual support should be shown.

Now let us consider what steps you can take to help your son who is bullying.

- Initially, you must discuss the matter with your son. Endeavour to get him to understand the negative effects his behaviour is having on his sister and the whole family.

- If your discussion with your son does not result in a change of behaviour, it is vital to seek help from outside. Consult your family doctor and ask that he be referred to the appropriate service. You will have to do all you can to convince your son to avail of the service. This may be a difficult task for you. Your family doctor or someone you know he trusts and loves may help you encourage him to do so.

- If he will not accept help, another possible method of treatment would be for the whole family to attend family therapy and all members could be encouraged to work together to help your son to develop more positive behaviour.

- Do all you can to make him feel involved with the family in a positive way. Include him in decision making. Ask him to do little favours for you. Try, in an informal way, to get him talking about what might be disturbing him and causing him to bully his sister. Maybe he just needs to be reassured of your interest, love and concern.

Question My personal life is being destroyed by a bully at work. Unfortunately my family is suffering too because I come home every evening feeling in bad form. Can you advise me what to do?

Answer The negative effects of workplace bullying do not stay in the workplace when you leave it. You carry them home with you. Victims of workplace bullying have told me that they tend to be morose and withdrawn at home and they argue with their partners and children. They tend to watch television without any real concentration, feel extremely exhausted and show little interest in food. They do not have the energy or interest to go to their local for a drink. They find it difficult to sleep and spend long hours recalling every detail of the bullying experience at work. If this is happening to you, it may be difficult for your family to understand but it is important for you to communicate your feelings to your husband, wife or partner so that they can give you support. It is important for you to share your story with as many caring relatives and friends as possible.

Do not bury all these negative emotions within you. It may be therapeutic for you to say how you feel. It is important for you to visit your family doctor and be open with them. Ask your family doctor to direct you to a stress management seminar and to a counsellor. Your health is your greatest wealth and you must protect it. Eventually, in your own good time, when you have built up your psychological strength, you should take all the steps to confront your bully.[5]

(See pages 38–46 for ways of confronting the bully in your workplace.)

Question   I feel unable to cope with the constant and aggressive demands made by my children for expensive designer label clothes, shoes and so on that I cannot afford. I feel bullied by my children. Have you any suggestions to help me with the problem?

Answer   This is a problem experienced by many parents. The family is part of society and is affected by it. Our society is a consumer one. Bullying will inevitably take place in a consumer society where people are motivated to believe that what they want is what they need. This is brought about and intensified by the aggressive marketing we see all around us. Luxury commodities are dangled before our eyes through manipulative advertisements in newspapers, magazines and on radio, television and the Internet. Children are quick to get the message!

Teenagers who do not have fashionable and expensive clothing and accessories or exotic hairstyles can be ridiculed and bullied by their peers. This can motivate them to bully their parents for money to buy these expensive items. Perhaps you need to increase your efforts to help your children to have a sense of responsibility. They must be made to realise that money has to be earned and that the commodities they demand do not top the list of priority needs in the home.[6]

To be practical, may I suggest that you:

- invite your children to sit down with you to discuss the family budget and see what money is available for the essentials in the home and what is available for non-essentials;

- discuss with them what money they can earn themselves without disrupting their studies and how their earnings can help to buy the non-essentials they want.

It has been noticed that teenagers can be quite reasonable in financial matters when they are invited to participate in the running of the home and not just treated as lodgers.[7]

Question   My 42-year-old brother is being bullied
           by his wife. How do you think he could
           be affected by this bullying? How do you
           think I could help him?

Answer   It is difficult to know how your brother is
           being affected by the bullying experience.
           Some men cope better than others and
           many men are not able to cope at all. Much
           will depend on the loving support you and
           others can give to your brother.

           As a sister, you must be careful to make
           it clear to your brother that you do not want
           to interfere in his marital problems but that
           you are ready to support him. Make it clear
           to him that you do not want to probe into
           the private and intimate affairs of what is
           going on between himself and his wife.

           Your brother may not be ready or able to
           discuss how he really feels because of his
           painful experience. He may want to cut
           himself off from all social contacts. Do not
           force him to communicate his negative
           feelings but tell him that you are there for
           him and that you, as his loving sister, are
           ready to listen. Assure him of your confi-
           dentiality. He may be tearful and, if he is,
           tell him that being tearful with people he
           trusts can be therapeutic. However, advise
           him to try to avoid crying in front of his
           bullying wife because that may be inter-
           preted as weakness. Your brother may
           suffer from a poor self-image and a loss of
           confidence. You can help him by praising
           him for the good things he does for others
           and for his good qualities. You can help him
           articulate how he feels by asking him
           questions such as, "Are you sleeping

properly at night? Do you feel anxious?"
Encourage him to talk about his feelings of
being trapped at home in the bullying
situation. If your brother is tending to lose
concentration or seeking solace from the
excessive use of alcohol, tobacco or other
substances, then you can conclude that the
negative effects of the bullying should be a
matter for concern. It would be wise to
advise him to visit his family doctor and if at
all possible to have counselling.

Question   My wife and I have been in conflict for some time. As a result of this conflict she is becoming more aggressive and is bullying me. What do you think I can do to solve the problem?

Answer   You and your wife must be suffering tremendously in your home where there is little harmony and peace. Both of you must do something to solve this problem before it destroys your lives. It might be helpful for you to reflect on some of the following ideas about conflict and how to address it.

Conflict exists when two or more people perceive that their interests are incompatible and express hostile attitudes or take action that damages the ability of the other party to pursue their interests. Conflict is the by-product of living together with our differences. Many people do not realise that conflict is a common experience in homes. The vast majority of people experience conflict in their homes. In a time of conflict, we often do the wrong thing by panicking.

Most people want to communicate well in their homes but unfortunately, many have never learned to communicate when it counts most, i.e. in conflict. Conflict is the midwife of growth in relationships.[8] If it is handled badly, it can destroy relationships but if it is handled well, relationships can grow and deepen through it. Knowing how to handle conflict is essential in every home and it can help to avoid bullying situations.

When we are addressing conflict we may react, which means we shout, blame, lose our temper and explode. This does not solve the conflict in any way. We can instead respond by saying something like, "So we have a difference of opinion. Let us recognise each other's feelings in this matter. Can we do so calmly, attentively and with respect for each other? Let us see how we can find other ways of handling our difference of opinion." Responding rather than reacting is the best way to do so. It would be wise for you to ask yourself regularly, "When I am in conflict with my wife do I react or do I respond?"

It might be helpful for you to analyse the main outcomes of conflict in the home: escalation, invalidation, and avoidance and withdrawal.

Escalation
Escalation is when matters are exaggerated and blown out of all proportion. Escalation can start with a simple observation such as, "This house is becoming very untidy". That simple observation can precipitate a nasty response such as, "Oh, for heaven's sake, give me a break! You are far too fussy! It is getting impossible to live with you. I am doing my best and my best is not good enough. I do not know why I stay in this house at all!"

When there is escalation, a comment can be made that hurts the other person tremendously, especially if it relates to something that was said in confidence in more intimate times. A cycle of returning negative comments for negative comments continues.

How can you handle escalation?
Try what is known as short-circuiting: soften your tone of voice and try to acknowledge

the other person's point of view. Another tip would be to call for "time out". If you feel things are getting out of control, just stop talking for a moment and enjoy a cup of tea or spend a few minutes looking at the television together.

Invalidation
Invalidation is when one person subtly or directly puts down the thoughts, feelings or character of the other. Such behaviour is a perfect example of bullying and can painfully lower the self-esteem of the targeted person. People naturally cover up their innermost feelings when they believe they will be put down and bullied.

Research has shown that invalidation plays a significant part in conflict and bullying in the home. It is like a poison that kills off peace and serenity within the family.

How can you avoid invalidation?
Respecting each other's character and feelings are the best ways of avoiding invalidation. The person raising the concern should be respected and heard. Remember, you do not have to agree with the person in order to validate their feelings. Validation is a powerful tool that one can use both to build relationships at home and to prevent es-calation and bullying. However, it takes great self-control to validate someone, especially if one is angry or frustrated, but it is well worth a try.

Withdrawal and avoidance
Withdrawal happens when one person shows an unwillingness to get into or stay

with an important discussion. For example, getting up and leaving the room or by saying something like, "Leave me alone. I heard it all before".

Avoidance is simply preventing the conversation from happening in the first place. The person trying to avoid talking will always find an excuse: for example, "I can't meet with you at that time. I have another commitment that I can't change" or "I'm tired now. I'll do it later". Later seldom comes! This is a hidden form of bullying if it persists over a period.

There is often a process of one person pursuing the problem and the other withdrawing. When it comes to the process of *pursue* and *withdraw* it becomes like a dance – *pursue/withdraw, pursue/withdraw*. Studies show that men tend to withdraw more frequently with women tending to pursue. However, in many situations the pattern is reversed. Withdrawal and avoidance can be very destructive. They are key factors in creating unhappiness in a home and can lead to bullying behaviour.

How can you avoid withdrawal and avoidance?
Realise that the problem will get worse if you allow the withdrawal and avoidance to continue, because the pursuer will pursue more and more and the withdrawer will withdraw more and more. Besides, when issues are important it should be obvious that trying to avoid dealing with them only makes matters worse and the bullying behaviour may be intensified. You cannot stick your head in the sand and pretend the

problem is not there. Keep in mind that you and your spouse/partner are not independent of each other; you need each other and your family needs you both. In a firm and gentle manner, you must continue to request that your spouse/partner discusses the problem with you. Whatever happens, avoid allowing yourself to adopt any bullying tactics.

Recovery is always a slow process but if you make sure your approach is correct then the end results may be favourable.

Negative interpretations

Negative interpretations occur when one person consistently believes that the motives of the other person are more negative than is really the case: for example, "You purposely came home late to annoy me", whereas the other person may have been genuinely delayed. This kind of interpretation is very destructive, makes conflict much harder to deal with constructively and can lead to bullying behaviour. To say something like, "I get very upset when you come home late" would be a much more constructive statement to make.

What is the solution to negative interpretations?

Look for evidence to the contrary. For example, the person who thinks negatively could ask questions such as:

- Do they do things for me that I like?

- Am I feeling sorry for myself?

- Do I think of myself as a martyr?

Focus on feelings

I cannot emphasise enough that the most important contributory factor in helping to avoid bullying in the home is the willingness to recognise the feelings of the other. All of us have an innate desire to have our feelings recognised. In discussions to solve a problem, the temptation is often to look for a solution without paying due attention to the feelings of the other. It is vitally important that during discussions you enter into and understand the thoughts, concerns and feelings of each other. How often have we all discovered that after an excellent discussion there is really no problem to be solved? This is because very often in our relationships we want much more than solutions to problems.

During my many years in pastoral work, I have asked couples in difficult situations, "What do you want from your relationship?" The majority gave an interesting reply. Did they want emotional security? No! Financial security? No! A beautiful home? No! Such things were not excluded from their desires but the greatest desire of the majority of the couples was that their spouse/partner would be a friend. When the same couples were asked what they understood by a friend they replied, "A friend is someone who listens, who understands, who appreciates, who forgives, who recognises feelings." This is the kind of good listening we need when we are discussing a problem. Very often, what we want most in our homes when we are upset is not so much the reaching of an agreement or even change, but just to feel heard and understood.

Of course, to be heard and understood is the essence of good constructive discussion and vital in the process of dealing with conflict and avoiding bullying. However, it must be recognised that there will be many times when your discussion will naturally lead to the next step, i.e. working together to find a solution.

Problem solution
Presuming you have a good discussion during which you have had some success in hearing and understanding each other's feelings, you now move on to the next step: *problem solving.* Your discussion will no doubt have taken you through many issues of concern. Now you need to know what is the issue on which you must focus your attention. Often problems in a home seem insurmountable, but when they are broken down, they become more manageable.

Brainstorming
For you to work together in a practical way, a good process to try would be brainstorming. To do this you sit together, both of you make suggestions as to what you could do to solve the problem and one of you writes down the suggestions. If brainstorming is to be effective, you must follow the rules of the game:

• Make any kind of suggestions, no matter how crazy they may seem. As they are mentioned, write them down.

• Be very creative in your suggestions.

• Do not evaluate the suggestions during the

brainstorming – either verbally or non-verbally through body language.

- Do not comment critically. If you do not criticise, you will encourage each other to come up with great ideas.

- Be light-hearted because this is a time when you can have some fun.

Wonderful solutions can emerge from the ideas made during a brainstorming session. Exhaust all your ideas before you decide which of them you will work on first. Following these rules will help you resist the tendency to decide prematurely on a solution that is not the best you can find.

Agreement and compromise
Your aim in the brainstorming exercise is to reach an agreement and compromise. That means to come up with a specific solution or combination of solutions on which you both agree. When you reach an agreement, you must promise each other to apply that which you have agreed. It may be easy to see the value of *agreement* but you may have trouble with the idea of *compromise*. To some it may sound like all win or lose. Compromise is simply giving up something you wanted in order to reach an agreement. It is a question of give and take. No one gets everything they want. The goal is to help you win as a team, with solutions that show your mutual care and respect and that bring you closer together. In the process, you may have to give up of yourself but if you can do so then, as a couple and as a family, the effort will have been worthwhile.

Follow-up

If you have come to an agreement and compromise, do not forget to arrange a follow-up. If you fail to do this, there will be the danger that nothing will happen and all your previous work on discussion and sharing will have been in vain. You must plan to check on yourselves. Remember the old saying, "If you fail to plan you plan to fail". It is so important for you to set a specific time (in a week or a month) to sit down and see how well the agreement is working and to discuss any small changes needed to help it work better.[9]

Many couples have found this method of dealing with conflict helpful. There is no reason why it should not help you too. It is an excellent preventative measure in terms of avoiding bullying.

Question   **My husband has been bullying me for a number of years and I need help. I do not know what to do. Can you suggest where I can get help?**

Answer   There are many organisations that can provide you with the assistance you need and deserve. The following are some of the resources for addressing relationship problems in home life:

- The Support for Families Directory is published by the Department of Social, Community and Family Affairs. It contains the names, addresses and telephone numbers of a wide variety of support groups and counselling services throughout the Republic of Ireland. Contact: The Department of Social, Community and Family Affairs, Family Unit, Aras Mhic Dhiarmada, Dublin 1, Tel: (01) 7043000. Website: www.welfare.ie

- Accord – Marriage Counselling Service: Central Office, Tel: (01) 5053112, Fax: (01) 6016410, Email: admin@accord.ie, Website: www.accord.ie; Northern Ireland Administration Office, Tel: (028) 90-233002, Fax: (028) 90-328113. Email: accordni@tinyworld.co.uk Website: www.accord.co.uk

- Personal Counselling Institute (PCI): Tel: (01) 2807888, Fax: (01) 4642060. Email: pci@oceanfree.net Website: www.pcicounselling.com

- Marriage and Relationships Counselling Service (MRCS): Tel: (01) 6785256.
  Fax: (01) 6785260.
  Email: mrcs@eircom.net
  Website: www.mrcs.ie

- Church of Ireland Marriage Council:
  Tel: (01) 4978422.
  Email: sandra.massey@rcbdub
  Website: www.marriagecouncil.Anglican.org

- Family Life Service: Tel: (053) 23086.
  Fax (053) 23125.
  Email: flswexford@eircom.net

- Anne Dempsey: Tel: (01) 8274503.
  Email: annedempsey@eircom.net

- Muriel O'Toole, PBVM: Tel: (0502) 62101

- Frances Heery: Tel: (044) 47395.
  Email: fheery@indigo.ie

- Jean Casey: Tel: (01) 8370433.
  Email: jeancasey@eircom.net

- Turning Point Inclusion: Tel: (01) 2807888/
  (01) 2800626, Fax: (01) 2800643.
  Email: info@turningpoint.ie

- Family Life Centre: Tel: (071) 9663000,
  Fax: (071) 9662954.
  Email: info@familylifecentre.ie
  Website: www.familylifecentre.ie

- Tara Counselling and Personal Development Centre: Tel: (082) 82-250024.
  Fax: (082) 82-250023.
  Email: info@taraomagh.com
  Website: www.taraomagh.com

Question   **I am a widow and I am advanced in years. I fear the future because I have heard horrific stories of how old people have been bullied by their families and in retirement homes. Can you advise me what to do to secure my future?**

Answer   In the Irish traditional society, elderly people were valued and appreciated. The old were associated with wisdom, experience, culture, links with the past and folklore. Reverence and respect were shown to grandparents, great-grandparents and elderly uncles and aunts. Unfortunately, there is a tendency in modern times for that to change.

My pastoral experience over many years has convinced me that bullying of the elderly is far too common in our society. It is very painful for the elderly but also very upsetting for those of us who observe it happening in families and retirement homes.

Bullying can make the aged feel miserable, sad and rejected. Bullies can deprive the elderly of their physical, emotional and human needs. The sad fact is that this bullying behaviour is often done by relatives who refuse to communicate with them about their finances, news of relatives and old friends. Bullies inflict horrific pain on the elderly by ridiculing them about very personal matters, such as their uncoordinated body movements, inability to climb stairs, lack of colour co-ordination in dress, memory failure, speech difficulties and incontinence. One of the cruellest forms of bullying is forcing the elderly to hand over ownership of their homes or forcing them to change their wills. Some retirement homes can exploit the elderly by refusing to admit them unless they hand over ownership of their homes to the retirement home. This would seem most unjust because in many cases the life span of the elderly can be very limited.

I can understand how you fear getting older, but there is no need to be afraid of the future if you make good plans to ensure you will enjoy happiness in your later years. The future for all of us is very unsure but it is most important to make provisions while you are well and while your mental faculties are sound. Prevention is better than cure. To avoid difficulties in your golden years, it is advisable for you to consult a solicitor to ensure that your will is in order, your savings secure and that someone is given the power of attorney in the event of you not being mentally or physically capable of handling your financial affairs, home and property.

Elderly people sometimes allow relatives or friends to share their home with them. This can lead to difficulties and even bullying behaviour if there are no legally binding agreements made so that the elderly owner of the house is protected in terms of their privacy and space. Care has to be taken so that the owner does not become a cheap housemaid or a babysitter.

Endnotes

1. Andrea Adams with Neil Crawford (2000) *Bullying at Work*, London: Virago Press, pp. 71–4.
2. Consultation with Marie Murray (29 July 2003).
3. Kate Kelly (2003) *Stopping Bad Behaviour*, London: Contemporary Books, pp. 70–1.
4. Ré Ó Laighléis (1996) *Ecstasy*, Dublin: Poolbeg Press Ltd, pp. 95–104.
5. David Graves (2002) *Fighting Back*, London: McGraw-Hill Companies, p. xx.
6. Tony Byrne, CSSp (1998) *Working for Peace and Justice*, Ndola, Zambia: Mission Press.
7. Consultation with consultant psychiatrist Dr Nuala Healy (12 August 2003).
8. Paulo Freire and Antonio Faundez (1989) *Learning to Question*, New York: Continuum Publishing Company, p. 2.
9. Howard Markham, Stanley Schott and Susan L. Blumberg (1994) *Fighting for your Marriage*, San Francisco, USA: Jossey-Bass Publishers, pp. 63–6.

Part III

BULLYING IN THE SCHOOL

Dr Brendan Byrne

Question   **How can we recognise bullying at school?**

Answer   It is important to keep a sense of balance in any discussion of bullying behaviour. There will always be name-calling, slagging and teasing. However, when a line is crossed it can be devastating for the person affected by it. The age-old excuse, "We were only messing" needs to be constantly challenged, especially in schools. The behaviour becomes bullying when the same person(s) is repeatedly on the receiving end of negative attention, against their wishes, and is unable to prevent it. The Department of Education and Science *Guidelines on Countering Bullying Behaviour in Primary and Post-Primary Schools*, published in September 1993, define bullying as: "Repeated aggression, verbal, psychological or physical, conducted by an individual or a group against others."[1]

A further useful definition is to see bullying as an abuse of power. This means anyone is capable of bullying in certain situations. A parent could bully a child; one student could bully another student; a teacher could bully a student; and one student or group of students could bully a teacher. A boy of sixteen put it in frightening terms when he described bullying as *the breaking down of a person.*

Question   **How can a person be bullied?**

Answer   An examination of a bullying incident will
often focus on whether it is physical or
mental, or a combination of both. While the
common view of bullying is that it is usually
physical, the reality is different. Most bullying
takes the form of slagging, jeering, name-
calling, teasing and the deliberate
provocation of the victim. Slagging is a wide-
ranging term that can be used to describe
everything from comments about physical
appearance and clothes, to remarks about
sexual orientation. At the level of harmless
banter, a person's haircut could be the focus
of attention. Much more hurtful and
damaging could be comments about a
person's physical appearance, e.g. big ears,
a big nose, large or small size.

Boys engage in two particularly upsetting
forms of slagging. The first is where a person
is called "queer", "bent" or "gay". This can
start very simply: perhaps there is a boy in
Second Year of secondary school whose
voice has not broken; maybe a boy looks
somewhat effeminate or is not very skilful
at the sport played by the majority of the
boys; somebody calls him "Rosie" or
"Sheila"; he is seen to become very upset;
this becomes a source of fun, so the name
sticks. Imagine the effect if this persists for
one or two years or even longer.

The second form of slagging particularly
common among boys is where remarks are
made about a person's mother, sister or
girlfriend, often with a sexual innuendo.

In some cases, malicious rumours are
started. This is especially common among

girls, where comments are made about a person's sexual behaviour and terms such as "slut" and "slag" are used.

Sometimes, a former best friend can be the source of a very hurtful form of bullying. This happens when they are not content to let the relationship end. They may systematically turn others against the former friend, thereby isolating them. Information of a personal or confidential nature that was shared in the course of the friendship is now disclosed to others. There is a double loss because of a sense of betrayal in addition to the loss of a friend.

Question   **What makes a person a victim or a bully?**

Answer   Anybody can become the focus of bullying.
Whether or not someone is bullied depends
on their level of vulnerability in a given
situation and the reaction they give when it
happens. In considering what may increase
a person's level of vulnerability, these are
some risk factors:

- physical characteristics;

- personality traits;

- family background;

- changes in family circumstances;

- atmosphere in the school.

A child's physical characteristics may
attract attention – anything from hair colour
to size. There are ways to counter this. One
is to ensure that your child feels good – give
them plenty of positive messages about
appearance. Do not deny the obvious if it
comes up – you will lose credibility. Point
out that everybody has distinguishing
features, which is what makes us unique. It
is equally important, however, to build up
emotional resources. Help them to understand that the reason why they are being
treated like this may be jealousy or insecurity
on the part of the bully.

The second trait to look out for in your
child is shyness or sensitivity. There is no
doubt that the shy, sensitive child is the one
most at risk. While sensitivity is an asset in
many situations, in this context it can make
a person more vulnerable to negative
treatment.

The third risk should not be seen as a criticism of parents, because it is through our children that we are most vulnerable. However, if a parent is over-protective, this may pass on a certain level of anxiety to the child. The ideal is to find the balance so that your child will speak openly to you if they are under pressure and yet know that they will not have to face a detailed inter-rogation every day after school.

Illness, bereavement or loss of employ-ment can alter family circumstances in a dramatic way and may lead to increased vulnerability.

The final and perhaps the most important consideration when assessing the bullying risk to your child is the atmosphere in the school. What are the school authorities prepared to tolerate? Is there a policy on bullying and, if so, what is it? When schoolyard banter turns nasty, personal or sexual, how is that handled by the staff? Are messages of tolerance and respect being communicated to the children?

It is a difficult proposition to alter the atmosphere in the school. Atmosphere is such an intangible thing. Prevention is always better than cure. It is necessary to create an atmosphere where it is acceptable to talk to someone if you are being bullied or if you know that someone else is. We need to give individuals and groups the confidence and strategies to be able to deal with bullying. People who bully need help to find an alternative way of behaving.

Question   **Why do people bully?**

Answer   It is now generally accepted that bullying is
a learned behaviour; nobody is born a bully.
The bullying behaviour develops when early,
negative attempts to assert control are
rewarded. If children attain power, status
and control by bullying other children, it
takes a powerful argument to change that.

A major complication in dealing with
bullying behaviour is that people can be both
bully and victim, the so-called bully–victim,
depending on the circumstances. If aggression, either physical or verbal, is the norm
at home, that behaviour is likely to be
modelled. It is my belief that the impact of
verbal aggression is often underestimated.
Children receiving negative messages about
themselves may displace these feelings by
bullying somebody weaker and more
vulnerable than they are.

In discussing why some people bully,
there is a danger that a difficult home
background will always be used to explain
the behaviour. However, this is not always
so. Some of the worst examples of bullying
that I have come across have been carried
out by people from very advantaged back-
grounds. Jealousy is one of the main causes
of bullying and crosses all boundaries of
class, gender and personality.

Bullies are generally children who have
no sense of empathy with the pain and
suffering of others. However, they can learn
to have empathy with their targets if the
situation is handled early and sensitively.
The sooner you can make them aware of
the damage they are causing, the better.

Perception is important: one child's banter is another child's bullying. The key here is the perception of the victim. If the behaviour is causing persistent distress and yet the bully continues, that is bullying.

Question   What do people say about bullying?

Answer   One of the most important human needs is
the need for inclusion. The worst part of
bullying is the loneliness. One adult to whom
I spoke recalled the following about his time
in school:

> When I went into secondary school, I found
> it difficult to adjust to the new situation. By
> second year, I was being subjected to name-
> calling with a mental or obscene connotation
> "Weirdo", "Queer", "Mental". I found it
> disturbing and distressing. I began to
> internalise and personalise these things.
> Over a period, my mind stopped working, just
> as if somebody had taken the power out of
> it. My energy went – physically, mentally,
> every way. Eventually, I became locked into
> a role. I was perceived as freakish, peculiar,
> queer. I began to play their game, to give
> them what they expected. My self-confidence
> and self-esteem were so badly affected that
> I began to doubt myself. I was so distressed,
> traumatised and hurt that I was rendered
> literally speechless about what was hap-
> pening to me. I felt wounded. I used to cry
> and cry on my own at home and even on
> holidays. I felt like someone was beating
> down on my heart with a hammer.[2]

A boy of seventeen described how this kind
of situation could evolve:

> The bully is a highly strategic person. Using
> his/her tactical methods he/she is able to
> locate the victim's Achilles heel and hammer
> home on this. In the case of mental bullying,
> the bully lowers the self-esteem of the victim,
> and that makes him/her feel worthless.
> Speaking from personal experience, even if
> the bullying stops, the victim still carries the

mark, being extremely self-aware and self-critical.[3]

Young people have a well-developed sense of what bullying behaviour is. The following statements from a group of fifteen-year-olds illustrate this:

> I think it's bad and you feel sorry for the people who are bullied and sometimes you do it to go along with the class so you won't be slagged.
> Bullying is not just a form of physical abuse but also mental abuse and can really affect a person's life.
> Sometimes you are luckier if you are actually physically hurt, because then no one will call you a rat or anything. If you are just slagged, no one in your class seems to worry except really good friends – if you have any left.

The last statement highlights the fact that most bullying is verbal rather than physical. The danger of longer term bullying is that the person being bullied may build a barrier to keep the bully out, but they may end up keeping everybody else out as well. In this way they become an even easier target.

Question   **How can you prove you are being bullied?**

Answer   A major difficulty is trying to prove certain types of bullying. In my work as a counsellor, a student may ask, "How do you prove that when you walk into a room everybody stops talking? How do you prove that that person started a rumour about you, or wrote that on the back of a door?"

The answer is that it is virtually impossible to prove these things in a legal fashion. The emphasis needs to be much more on creating an atmosphere where it is safe to speak out if you are being bullied or, as part of the group observing such behaviour, to feel confident about letting it be known that you do not agree with it. We need to move from a position of responding to incidents of bullying to one of working proactively to preventing such behaviour. It needs to be acknowledged that we may never eradicate bullying behaviour. The challenge is to reduce the incidence to the lowest possible level.

Question   **Does bullying only happen in schools?**

Answer   Until relatively recently, bullying was considered a behaviour most common in schools. However, it is clear now that bullying happens in many different contexts. It can happen in the neighbourhoods where people live, in youth and sports clubs, in the workplace and in the home.

Question   **Where does bullying happen in schools?**

Answer   In primary schools, about three-quarters of all bullying takes place in the playground or yard. The reasons for this are varied. Some of the behaviour may stem from boredom or a desire to "have fun". At times, it may be orchestrated by a gang. It can range from verbal to physical or even a combination of both. It can range from so-called messing to the most insidious persecution.

Bullying can also occur in corridors, cloakrooms and toilets. It is done out of sight of adults, usually in such a way as to cause maximum humiliation to the victim. It can happen between classes; it can also occur in class when the teacher is not watching, for example when they are writing on the board. It is usually subtle – looks, glances and sniggers. It may be in written form or in the form of drawings.

There are increasing reports of mobile phone text messages being used to intimidate/bully people. It can involve everything from negative comments about physical appearance to physical threats.

Question   **What is the incidence of bullying in Irish schools?**

Answer   In October 1996, the results of a nationwide survey, funded by the Gulbenkian Foundation and the Department of Education and Science and completed by O'Moore, Kirkham and Smith of the Anti-Bullying Research and Resource Centre at Trinity College, Dublin, were released.[4] The study was carried out during the 1993/1994 school year with young people from eight years of age in primary schools up to Sixth Year in secondary schools completing questionnaires. Some 531 schools were involved – 320 primary and 211 secondary. This represented 10 per cent of all primary schools and 27 per cent of all post-primary. The study found that 1 in 20 primary school children and 1 in 50 at post-primary level were subjected to frequent (serious) peer bullying. The number of pupils being bullied who would not tell anyone in school increases with age, from 54 per cent of Third Class pupils to 74 per cent of Sixth Class pupils. In secondary schools, the level of non-reporting is as high as 92 per cent. The figures for telling someone at home show that in post-primary schools in Sixth Year, 80 per cent of pupils said they had not done so. At primary level, in Sixth Class, the number is 54 per cent. The survey also indicated that bullying in post-primary schools happens most in First and Second Year.

In their book *The ABC of Bullying*, Marie Murray and Colm Keane reported that 20 per cent of children are afraid to go to school because of bullying.[5] Byrne, in his study of schools in 1992, discovered an overall incidence of 10.4 per cent of children involved in bullying behaviour, with 5.3 per cent as bullies and 5.1 per cent as victims. He also found that boys were more likely to be involved as bullies than girls (only 25.7 per cent of bullies were girls).[6]

Question **How does the incidence of bullying in Irish schools compare to other countries?**

Answer For comparison, we will look at England and Wales, Norway and Australia. In a study carried out in Sheffield in 1993 by Whitney and Smith, it was found that bullying was extensive. Of primary school pupils, 27 per cent reported being bullied "sometimes" or more frequently and this included 10 per cent who were bullied "once a week" or more. For secondary schools, these figures were 10 per cent and 4 per cent respectively. Analyses by year group confirmed that there was a fairly steady decrease in reports of bullying from eight through to sixteen years. As far as reporting taking part in bullying others was concerned, this was admitted by some 12 per cent of primary school pupils "sometimes" or more frequently, including 4 per cent who bullied "once a week" or more frequently. For secondary schools, these figures were 6 per cent and 1 per cent respectively.[7] In Norway, Dan Olweus, who is considered the pioneer in research into bullying in schools, carried out a large-scale survey in 1983. He found that some 15 per cent of the students in primary and lower secondary schools corresponding to ages seven through sixteen in Norway were involved in bully/victim problems with some regularity, as either bullies or victims. Approximately 9 per cent, or 52,000 students, were victims and 7 per cent, or 41,000, bullied other students regularly. Some 5 per cent of the students were involved in more serious bullying problems, occurring "about once a week" or more frequently.[8] In Australia, research by Rigby and Slee discovered that among students aged eight to eighteen years, 20.7 per cent of boys and 15.7 per cent of girls reported being bullied at least once a week. There was a significant increase when children moved from primary to secondary school in Australia.[9]

Question **Is there a connection between bullying and suicide?**

Answer When a person commits suicide, there are usually a number of factors involved. It is impossible to say that there is a direct link between bullying and suicide. However, there is no doubt that bullying is a factor in some suicides. Severe bullying that has gone on for a long period may lead to feelings of anger and sadness, which may in turn lead to suicidal ideation (thoughts of suicide). It is certain that bullying leads to feelings of humiliation and a lowering of self-worth. In these circumstances, it is more likely that a person will consider suicide. For this reason, bullying must be approached in a very serious way in schools, with a major emphasis on prevention.

Question   **How was bullying dealt with in the past?**

Answer   Earlier it was stated that in 1993, the Depart-
                 ment of Education and Science published
                 the *Guidelines on Countering Bullying
                 Behaviour in Primary and Post-Primary
                 Schools.* Until then, there was no uniformity
                 in approach. Some schools had very
                 effective procedures, while in others there
                 was no agreed approach. The most com-
                 mon weakness was that there were no
                 preventative measures in place. It was only
                 when bullying occurred or came to light that
                 a decision was made as to what course of
                 action to take.

Question **What is in the** *Guidelines on Countering Bullying Behaviour in Primary and Post-Primary Schools?*

Answer The introduction to the Guidelines emphasised "that the issue of bullying behaviour be placed in a general community context to ensure the cooperation of all local agencies in dealing appropriately with it".[10] It points out that "Bullying behaviour affects everyone in the classroom, in the school community and, ultimately, in the wider community."[11] In an attempt to prevent bullying, the Guidelines recommended "a school policy which includes specific measures to deal with bullying behaviour within the framework of an overall school code of behaviour and discipline".[12] Co-operation and consultation are emphasised:

> ... the managerial authority of each school in developing its policy to counter bullying behaviour must formulate the policy in co-operation with the school staff, both teaching and non-teaching, under the leadership of the principal, and in consultation with the parents and pupils. In this way, the exercise of agreeing what is meant by bullying and the resultant development of school-based strategies for dealing with it are shared by all concerned.[13]

In raising the awareness of bullying in the school community so that they are more alert to its harmful effects, schools could choose to have a staff day on the subject of bullying, complemented by an awareness day for pupils and parents/guardians.[14] Within the school, there should be definite procedures for dealing with incidents of bullying behaviour. Parents/guardians must also be informed of the appropriate person to whom they can make enquiries regarding incidents of bullying behaviour, which they might suspect, or that have come to their attention through their children or other parents/guardians.[15] The non-teaching staff should be encouraged to report any incidents of bullying behaviour to the appropriate teaching member of staff.[16] Serious complaints should be reported to the principal or deputy principal who could make contact with the parents/guardians if necessary.[17]

The Guidelines define bullying, describe different types of bullying and discuss the effects and outline signs and symptoms of bullying. There are sections about where bullying happens and the characteristics of bullying. The major part of the Guidelines considers prevention and the development of a school policy for dealing with bullying. The Guidelines say that pupils involved in bullying behaviour need ongoing assistance.[18]

In conclusion, the Guidelines refer to the desirability of the inclusion of a module on bullying behaviour in the pre-service training of teachers, which would be a positive step in alerting potential teachers to the problems caused by such behaviour. In addition, the Guidelines considered that the expansion of in-service courses to teachers on aspects of bullying behaviour would be of considerable benefit to the teaching profession in the process of raising awareness and developing techniques to deal with such behaviour.[19] The Guidelines are a most effective resource for schools in the whole area of countering bullying behaviour.

Question   **What is meant by a community approach to countering bullying in schools?**

Answer   Bullying can begin outside the school and be continued inside. For example, a person may initially be bullied on the journey to or from school and then be subjected to bullying within the school. In countering bullying, the school can be viewed as a most important part of a larger community. It is vital to consider the role of parents, non-teaching staff, school bus drivers, shop-keepers, doctors and the police.

Question   **What is a school policy on bullying and why should schools have such a policy?**

Answer   A school policy on bullying is an agreed procedure for recording, investigating and dealing with bullying behaviour. The process by which a policy has been developed is as important as the content, as it is necessary to ensure that each party's interest is represented. Therefore, the school policy on bullying should be the result of a collaborative approach, involving all members of the school community including teaching staff, non-teaching staff, parents and students.

Bullying affects the whole atmosphere in the school, making it difficult for students to concentrate and learn, and for teachers to do their work. Therefore, prevention of bullying should be a major part of the policy. The purpose of the policy is to protect all members of the school community from being bullied (including teachers and other people working in the school, students and parents). To quote the Department's Guidelines:

> The role of the school is to provide the highest possible standard of education for all its pupils. A stable secure learning environment is an essential requirement to achieve this goal. Bullying behaviour, by its very nature, undermines and dilutes the quality of education and imposes psychological damage. As such, it is an issue that must be positively and firmly addressed through a range of school-based measures and strategies through which all members of the school community are enabled to act effectively in dealing with this behaviour.[20]

Once finalised, the policy should be disseminated widely by means of booklets, newsletters, posters, notice boards and parent meetings.

Question   **What is an anti-bullying code?**

Answer   One of the cornerstones of any policy to counteract bullying is an anti-bullying code. The advantage of such a code is that it sends a clear message to students and parents that this behaviour is not tolerated. When something is written down, it has far more impact than an oral statement. It also removes the opportunity for people to say that they never knew the matter was taken so seriously. The anti-bullying code should also be the result of a consultative process between teachers, students and parents. The following is an example of a code:

> In our school, everybody is valued. Difference of any type – race, religion, appearance, personality, background or interests – does not make it acceptable to bully a person. We are all different – that is what makes us special. The people in this school have the right to be themselves, and have the responsibility to treat others as they would like to be treated. Silence allows people to suffer. We speak out when we know we should.[21]

Question   **What do parents need to know about a school policy?**

Answer   Parents need to know that:

- the school takes the issue of bullying behaviour seriously;

- there is an anti-bullying statement in the Code of Discipline;

- they have a responsibility to ensure that their son/daughter does not engage in this behaviour;

- the school does have a policy on bullying which was drawn up with reference to the Department of Education and Science *Guidelines on Countering Bullying Behaviour in Primary and Post-Primary Schools* (September 1993), i.e. there are procedures for preventing, investigating and dealing with incidents of bullying behaviour;

- in investigating incidents of bullying, it is the usual procedure to ask any student to write an account of what happened. This does not necessarily imply that a student has been involved in unacceptable behaviour;

- when the school has investigated and established that bullying behaviour has occurred, a written record will be kept of bullying incidents. These records are best kept on a standardised form;

- the school has a programme of support for those affected by bullying behaviour and for those involved as perpetrators of bullying behaviour;

- the school does impose sanctions in the event of serious bullying;

- they would feel confident about noticing the signs and symptoms of bullying behaviour. That they would make contact with the school quickly but would then give the school the opportunity to investigate the matter fully and professionally;

- advising young people to retaliate physically usually only makes the situation worse;

- they need to have confidence in and support for the procedures operated by the school. Early contact with the school is the best approach.

Question   **What sanctions can a school use in the event of bullying?**

Answer   Serious incidents of bullying should be recorded on an incident form (see overleaf). Such incidents may occur in the classroom or around the school. Incidents may be reported by pupils (involving themselves or others) or by parents (perhaps to a teacher in their capacity as a form tutor). An incident form should be uncomplicated. It should record the date, time, place and names of people involved and should include brief details of the incident. These written records are most useful should parents need to be contacted. In particularly serious cases, Boards of Management may find this information very important in deciding what course of action to take.

Students should be aware that if they were involved in bullying the following would happen:

1. if they are involved, they will be warned to stop;

2. if they do not, their parents will be informed;

3. if the incident is particularly serious, they may be suspended.

Incident Sheet

Day _____ **Date** _____

Time _____ **Place** _____

Names of pupils involved _____

Details of Incident _____

Action Taken _____

_____

Initials (of investigating teacher) _____

Question   **What procedures should be followed in investigating a case of bullying?**

Answer   The following procedure is recommended.

1. Speak separately to the person who appears to be bullying, the person who appears to be the victim and, if possible, somebody not directly involved but who saw what happened. It can be useful to get all those involved to write an account of what happened. This is best done in private.

2. If the teacher considers the incident serious, it should be written down on a bullying incident sheet (described previously) and reported to the deputy principal/principal.

3. The deputy principal/principal should make contact with the parents if they consider it necessary.

4. Teachers should confer with colleagues, particularly when difficult situations arise.

5. Speak to the bully and inform them firmly but in a non-aggressive manner that such behaviour will not be tolerated. Remind them of the existing anti-bullying code/policy, if one exists. Any other action(s) should form part of an overall anti-bullying policy.

6. The person who has been the victim of bullying should be kept informed of all developments after the incident(s) have been reported and of any further action that is going to ensue.

7. The teacher should assure the person who has been the victim of bullying of ongoing support and should encourage them to report any further attempts at intimidation. From time to time, the teacher could check discretely with the student how things are going.

Question   **What could lessons about bullying be like in secondary schools?**

Answer   Through the Social Personal and Health Education (SPHE) programme in the school, there exists an opportunity to raise awareness in a structured way. The teachers involved in SPHE could decide a programme for each year group in the school. An example of some lesson plans is shown below.

Intention
To raise awareness of what bullying is, how it can happen and to consider group and individual responsibilities. This can be achieved in a series of lessons. The approach should be preventative rather than a response to bullying behaviour. It is important to target First Year classes each year as early as possible in September. This material can then be used as a foundation for further work in Second and Third Year. These lessons could also be adapted to suit primary school pupils.

Materials
Teacher: flip chart and markers.
Students: pen and paper.

Step 1
Read a poem(s) on the subject of bullying.

Step 2
Ask students to write down their definition of bullying. Write examples on flip chart/ blackboard.

Ask students to write down the following definitions:

Bullying is an abuse of power.

Bullying is the breaking down of a person.

Step 3
Divide the class into random groups of three. Ask them to discuss what it could feel like to be bullied. List the feelings on flip chart/board.

Step 4
Write the following statements on the board and ask students to write them down:

People have a right to be who and what they are.

You can never see inside somebody else's head.

Get them to discuss these two statements (in the same groups). Take feedback. The intention here is to focus on how feelings may be hurt either physically or emotionally and to foster a tolerance of difference. This will become more obvious when they become more aware of the differences within the group in terms of appearance, personality, background and interests.

As a follow on, get the groups to talk about slagging, examining what is good and bad about it. Talk about the excuse, "We were only messing".

Step 5
Ask each student to write a description of what a bully is like. They could follow this with a drawing/cartoon.

Step 6
Ask the class for suggestions as to why people are bullied/bully. Take feedback.

Step 7
Explore sensitively the idea of a "provocative" behaviour but emphasise that while sometimes a person may contribute to a situation, most people who are bullied have done nothing to deserve negative treatment. Often, they are just in the wrong place at the wrong time or perhaps somebody may be jealous of them.

Step 8
Form new groups of three. Ask each group to discuss the causes of jealousy and to give actual examples. List feedback.

Step 9
Ask each student to write down (anonymously) one word to describe the atmosphere in the class. They should do this on a separate piece of paper and privately. Collect the pages and mix them up. Read out the words and invite reaction.

Step 10
Case studies: these could be taken from various books on bullying and form the basis for discussion.

Step 11
Form groups of five. The task is for each group to devise a code of behaviour for the class using the following format:

In our class:
We should ... ... (*about five recommendations*)
We should not ... ... (*about five recommendations*)

After discussion, the group should write out the code on a large page. A subsequent class could be spent taking all the examples and working them into a single code, which reflects the opinions of the class. This could then be typed up, laminated and placed in the classroom if the class stays in the one room. Alternatively, each student could be given a copy. The following is an example of such a code.

Behaviour Code
In our group ...

We should:
- include everybody;
- let everybody be themselves;
- have a laugh;
- stick together;
- listen;
- treat each other with respect;
- treat one another equally.

We should not:
- leave a person out;
- talk behind one another's backs;
- laugh at what people say (opinion);
- put people down or slag about certain things;
- cheat or be sly to one another;
- make sexist comments;
- let the laugh go too far.

While teachers could facilitate this exercise, the code is best when expressed in the words of the pupils. It then represents the feelings of the young people themselves. The code may be used periodically to promote discussion and raise awareness of the unacceptability of bullying behaviour.

Question   **What could lessons about bullying be like in primary schools?**

Answer   As in secondary schools, SPHE is also taught in primary schools. There is also a teaching package designed for primary schools, called the Stay Safe Programme. It aims to prevent child abuse by equipping parents and teachers with the knowledge and skills necessary to protect children in their care. The programme contains a section on bullying and a lesson component for work with pupils. It points out that "children who are victims of bullying often feel shame, guilt or a sense of failure because they cannot cope with the bully". The rules of the Stay Safe Programme seem particularly appropriate when dealing with bullying: "Say 'No' ", "Get away", "Tell and keep telling".

Circle time was an idea developed by Teresa Bliss and Jo Tetley in 1993.[22] It brings together teachers and children in an enjoyable atmosphere of co-operation. It is a time set aside each week when children and their teacher sit in a circle and take part in games and activities designed to increase self-awareness, awareness of others and to understand what is important to them and their friends. Circle time helps children learn how to express their feelings and it encourages greater tolerance between girls and boys. As children learn more about themselves and each other, a warm and supportive group atmosphere is built, along with improved relationships. Circle time is used by many teachers in primary schools and is a very effective way to increase awareness of how bullying can cause distress.

Question   **What about bullying in boarding schools?**

Answer   The fact that students in boarding school spend more time in the school environment increases the potential for bullying behaviour. This is not to imply that boarding schools have an increased incidence of bullying compared to day schools. However, it does mean that authorities in these schools may have to look carefully at ways of preventing bullying. There are practical reasons for this.

In the early part of their time in boarding school, new pupils may be more vulnerable because of the lack of close family support. Programmes such as a mentor programme help a lot in this context. Dormitories can be an area of specific concern. Schools tend to be very aware of this and ensure that students participate in a carefully structured programme of study and extra-curricular activities. Supervision tends to be a major feature of dormitories and is frequently based on a well-organised prefect and mentor system. There may also be occasions when a person's property becomes a focus of attention for the bully, though this may also happen in day schools, too. Finally, the fact that students in boarding schools spend a lot of time with the same people can lead to tensions and there can be the difficulty of finding private space.

Question   Are there Internet sites on school or child-related bullying?

Answer   The following is a list of some useful sites:

- **Bullying Online and The Anti-Bullying Campaign (UK)**
  www.bullying.co.uk

- **Bully On line**
  www.bullycide/child.htm

- **Bullying at School Information (Scotland)**
  www.scre.ac.uk/bully/

- **Cool Schools Programme. North Eastern Health Board**
  www.coolschoolbullyfree.ie

- **Kidscape (UK)**
  www.kidscape.org.uk/kidscape/

- **BullyB'ware (Canada)**
  www.bullybeware.com/

- **No Bully Organisation (New Zealand)**
  www.nobully.org.nz/

- **Anti-Bullying Network (Scotland)**
  www.antibullying.net/

- **Bullying – A Survival Guide (UK)**
  www.bbc.co.uk/education/bully/
  index.htm

- **Bullying in Schools and What to Do about it (Australia)**
  www.education.unisa.edu.au/bullying/

- **Maine Project Against Bullying (USA)**
  http://lincoln.midcoast.com/~wps/
  against/bullying.html

- **Miami High School Anti-Bullying Site (USA)**
  www.onthenet.com.au/~townsend/anti-bullying.htm

Question   **What is the role of the class teacher in dealing with bullying?**

Answer   In primary school, the class teacher has the opportunity to get to know children very well because they are with them every day and for the full day. In the post-primary situation, the teacher will see the class for about forty minutes at a time and that may not be even every day. Consequently, teachers at the younger level will usually have a better idea of the dynamic within the class.

Bullying rarely occurs overtly in front of a teacher in the classroom and most bullying is non-physical, which means that it will seldom be a straight-forward situation. By its very nature, bullying is a secret activity and while the bully likes and needs an audience, they will be very careful about the composition of that audience. In the class, it can take the form of sniggers, whispers and looks. Material about a student may be written or drawings may be produced.

All of this can go on in a very subtle way and while the teacher may sense that all is not well and that something nasty is going on, they may find it difficult to be certain – and even more difficult to prove it! Indicators that something is wrong could be tone of voice, gestures, demeanour of a possible victim and the reaction of bystanders. However, the child being bullied will often be reluctant to report anything. The fear of being described as a "rat" is a major deterrent to disclosure. If asked openly in front of others, the victim is unlikely to want to speak publicly, for fear of making things worse.

Unless it was an obvious case of bullying,

the teacher is best advised to proceed in a low-key manner. If the teacher knows the student, they could find an opportunity to speak to them privately. The most important thing is for the teacher to make the student aware of the ongoing support that is available.

Question   **What is the role of the form tutor?**

Answer   In secondary school, the form tutor has the advantage of knowing the class well and being in a position to offer support if necessary. A simple statement along the lines of, "If ever any student wants to speak to me, they always can; if I am busy when you come along, always come back."

It is not possible to promise confidentiality but, as the sense of trust develops, the teacher can help a student to develop strategies to deal with the negative behaviour and to report it, if that is what they want.

Question   **What is the role of the chaplain?**

Answer   Some schools, mainly community schools, have a full-time chaplain. The chaplain is usually a member of the pastoral care team in the school. Working closely with the form tutors and the guidance counsellor, the chaplain offers a line of support to students who may be under pressure.

Question **What is the role of the guidance counsellor?**[23]

Answer Too often in schools in the past, there was a perception that it was the role of the guidance counsellor to deal with almost all students involved in bullying situations. However, more recently, there has been a realisation that a whole-school approach to dealing with bullying brings the best results.

In this context, the guidance counsellor works with students most severely affected by bullying behaviour, be they bullies or victims. This is best done in consultation with class teachers, form tutors, the principal and the deputy principal. Effective communication between the guidance counsellor and the parties previously mentioned is vital. It is important that teachers originally involved in a case get feedback on progress, or lack of it, as this makes the teacher feel part of the process.

If the school is viewed as a community, its members have rights and responsibilities. In relation to bullying, the victim has a right to freedom from bullying behaviour and the bully must be made to take responsibility for their actions. Discussions with the bully and the victim can enable the counsellor to work towards achieving this. The bullies and the victims may need help on an ongoing, long-term basis. The investment of time on the part of the counsellor is immense. If too many people are to be helped, the system will soon become overloaded. Therefore, the counsellor should deal with the more serious cases.

Helping a student who is a victim of bullying behaviour

A student who is being bullied needs to be listened to in a supportive way. Space to talk about the situation and the attendant feelings must be available. Sufficient time should be set aside to elicit and validate feelings.

Assure the student that the problem lies with the bully. This helps to remove the guilt that many people feel when they are bullied. It can help to ask the student questions such as: "Did you ever wonder why that person feels the need to call you names/jeer you/ hit you? Would they treat you like that if they felt good about themselves? Perhaps they are jealous of you."

Low self-esteem can be a major factor in being bullied. You can help a student to develop self-esteem in the following ways: getting involved in activities; developing assertiveness; learning to feel good about appearance; practising visualisations; re-integrating with classmates.

Getting involved in as many activities both in school and outside can help. It does not really matter what the activity is. The intention should be to meet a range of personalities in a range of settings. Martial arts and self-defence can be very useful activities if the intention is right, i.e. to become assertive rather than aggressive.

I place a lot of emphasis on developing assertiveness, because I believe that if a person is anxious and nervous in their thoughts, it shows in their body language and even in their voice. The bully thrives in a situation where their negative behaviour goes unchallenged. Assertiveness can break the cycle. The usual advice given to a person being slagged or called names is either to ignore it or answer back. Unless it is ignored with confidence, the hurt can show all over a person's face or in their body language. Answering back without the verbal facility to do so can provide an even bigger laugh for the perpetrators. A good approach is to say to the person being bullied:

> When it starts tomorrow, I want you to turn around and pick out the one who does it worst of all. Stand very firmly on the ground and get your head and shoulders up and briefly look at the person and show on your face the expression, "I heard that and I don't like it". Do not look angry and do not stare, because this may give them the excuse to say, "What are you looking at?" Decide then whether to stay or to walk away.

Many young people will say that they do not have the confidence to do this. However, when a person does not resist bullying – when they seem to accept the maltreatment, they attract further negative attention. The guidance counsellor can help the student by encouraging them to develop more positive body language and by role-playing the bullying situation with them. The simple technique of looking at their face and eyes in a mirror while practising more assertive body language can be beneficial to the student.

Self-consciousness about appearance can make a person vulnerable to bullying. The guidance counsellor can reassure and help a person to feel good about their appearance. The same is true about perceived lack of ability – academic or otherwise. In addition to academic ability, there is a need to highlight all the other abilities people may have – musical, sporting, artistic and so on.

Simple visualisations may also help. In a negative situation, imagining a wall all around their head can help the victim block out hurtful comments/insults. Similarly, it is necessary to live in the present and not to dwell on what happened yesterday and what may happen tomorrow.

If a person has been bullied for a period of time, they may become very isolated. Confidence may be affected to the point where the student stops making any effort to remain part of the group. In time, the person may become an easy target and even be described as a "loner". Even former friends may be ignored. The more isolated a person becomes the more vulnerable they are. The guidance counsellor may be able to help the individual to build up confidence again to the point where they will take the risk to reach out to others. It may be necessary to be firm about the fact that it takes an effort and will not be easy.

Helping the bully
People who bully need help to change their behaviour. It is necessary to give them the opportunity to explain why they are behaving like this – they may not even have worked this out on a conscious level themselves. Because bullying is such a negative behaviour, it is necessary at all times to separate the behaviour from the person. It is a fact

that this behaviour, however objectionable to us, provides them with a pay-off. Therefore, it is important to offer alternative ways of behaving. This could include getting the person involved in some school activity or a position where they may enjoy some form of responsibility. It is sometimes the case that the tough, brash, negative behaviour of the bully is masking a weak, fragile, insecure person with low self-esteem. Speaking in confidence to the guidance counsellor may be the first opportunity the student has had to speak about their real feelings.

People who bully lack empathy. This enables them to inflict suffering on others without feeling remorse. The guidance counsellor can help such a person to develop a sense of empathy by talking about the effects of their behaviour, with the emphasis on feelings.

In some situations where the guidance counsellor has been working with the bully and the victim, it may be possible to bring the two parties together. However, this should only happen when the victim agrees and there is no danger of making the situation worse.

Sometimes, despite the best efforts of the guidance counsellor, there is no improvement or there may even be deterioration in the behaviour of the bully. In this situation, the issue needs to be referred back to the school policy on bullying. It is now once again a disciplinary matter involving sanctions and is part of the whole-school approach mentioned earlier.

Question   **Are teachers ever bullied?**

Answer   Anybody can find themselves the victim of
                a bully, and teachers are no exception.

> In essence, bullying is unwanted behaviour
> of a physical or verbal nature which unfairly
> discriminates, humiliates, embarrasses or
> intimidates an employee, or results in an
> employee feeling threatened, offended or
> compromised in any way. It is behaviour,
> which undermines the confidence and self-
> esteem of the person being bullied. Any level
> of staff, i.e. manager, supervisor or col-
> league, may perpetrate it.[24]

In the course of their professional duties,
teachers may be bullied by colleagues,
students, parents/guardians and non-
teaching staff. In the case of colleagues, the
bullying may involve rumours, exclusion
(from social events especially), intimidating
body language or interference with property.
Sometimes there may be an invasion of
personal space, for example where teachers
have lockers in close proximity to one
another.

The school principal may be the source
of the bullying. This can be a very difficult
situation for a teacher because of the abuse
of power involved. It can take many forms
including inappropriate confrontation
(sometimes in public), unfair treatment in
relation to timetabling or inappropriate
comments/questions about a teacher's
personal life or professional competence.
Principals can also be bullied. An individual
or sometimes a group of teachers may
refuse to co-operate with decisions. There
may be inappropriate comments to parents/

guardians or a lack of respect or courtesy. A principal appointed from within the staff may be the object of jealousy while a principal from outside the staff may face lack of co-operation. Whether any of this becomes bullying depends on the numbers involved and the degree of the negative treatment.

Parents/guardians can bully teachers by engaging in inappropriate questioning of a teacher's competence, authority or teaching methods either in person, in writing or on the telephone. The worst scenario is where a teacher is approached in a public way in the school without any prior arrangement. This is less common now, as schools are much more aware of procedures to benefit all members of the school community when such situations arise.

The non-teaching staff may on occasion bully or be bullied within the school, for example incidents involving school caretakers, secretarial staff, classroom assistants and "lollipop" women and men. Difficulties may arise in relation to access (to rooms and equipment), photocopying, the passing on of telephone messages and repair work. There may sometimes be friction between members of the teaching and non-teaching staff.

A teacher could also be bullied by students – an individual, a group, even an entire class of students can be involved. This behaviour could take the form of inappropriate language, gesture, insolence and non-cooperation. Teachers may be subjected to forms of sexual harassment through physical contact: for example, teachers, both male and female, could be harassed in a crowded corridor or lewd material could be written on a board.

Question   **What can teachers do if they are bullied?**

Answer   The first thing to do is to decide that the behaviour involved is bullying.

- Consider the motive of the perpetrator(s) – jealousy, power, control, fun.

- Keep a written record – details of when, where, who and what.

- Note such things as tone of voice, facial expression and appropriateness of subject matter and location.

- Examine ways in which they may have contributed to the situation.

Where to turn for assistance
In the light of recent legislation, it is highly advisable that a school should have a written policy on bullying and harassment in the workplace.

A written policy should state that:

- all workers have a right to a work environment which is free from sexual harassment and bullying;
- sexual harassment and bullying will not be condoned;
- a named member of staff has been designated to handle complaints of sexual harassment and bullying;
- procedures for dealing with complaints will be made known to all employees;
- complaints will be dealt with seriously, quickly and confidentially;
- a person who makes a complaint, or anyone who helps in the investigation of that complaint, will be protected from victimisation and retaliation;
- appropriate disciplinary measures will be taken if the complaint is proven.[25]

It is easier to get assistance in a school that has procedures as outlined above. There are a number of sources to which teachers could look for support.

• Someone they trust.

• The Employee Assistance Service. This service is available to primary, post-primary and retired teachers. A member of the assistance team is able to provide information and support, by listening in an understanding and non-judgemental way while seeking to help resolve personal and professional concerns. Any discussion with a member of the team is treated in the strictest confidence, except in a situation where there is danger to the individual or someone else or where the conceal-ment of information would compromise a member of the Employment Assistance team. The service is free of charge and available throughout the country.

• The school steward.

• The Anti-Bullying Centre in Trinity College. The centre provides advice, guidance and counselling for people affected by bullying. There is also a reference library.

• The Employment and Equality Agency, 36 Upper Mount Street, Dublin 2, Tel: (01) 6624577, offers advice and support.

Question   **Is bullying among teachers a bigger problem in certain schools?**

Answer   Bullying is more likely in schools that do not have an explicit policy on bullying behaviour. In an ideal situation, this should refer to all members of the school community. Procedures to be followed in the event of bullying should be publicised and known to all members of the school community.

It is generally accepted that a person's liability to being bullied is directly related to that person's level of vulnerability at that point in time. In the case of a teacher, the following factors may increase the likelihood of bullying:

- inexperience;

- insufficient support;

- lack of confidence, which can manifest itself through body language and tone of voice;

- lack of competence;

- personal difficulties, for example illness or recovery from illness and family difficulties;

- general atmosphere in the school, for example an all-round lack of respect; an acceptance of aggressive behaviour; a "macho" culture; or tolerance of sexist attitudes, especially in single-sex schools.

Question   **Do teachers ever bully?**

Answer   The Department of Education and Science
                 Guidelines, 1993, state that:

> A teacher may, unwittingly or otherwise,
> engage in, instigate or reinforce bullying
> behaviour in a number of ways:
>
> • using sarcasm or other insulting or
>   demeaning forms of language when
>   addressing pupils; making negative
>   comments about a pupil's appearance or
>   background;
> • humiliating, directly or indirectly, a pupil
>   who is particularly academically weak or
>   outstanding, or vulnerable in other ways;
> • using any gesture or expression of a
>   threatening or intimidatory nature, or any
>   form of degrading physical contact or
>   exercise.[26]

Teachers need to be aware of the impact of
their behaviour on the atmosphere in the
class group; they have a major responsibility
to be role models for positive behaviour.

Question   **Why do parents worry about bullying?**

Answer   In recent years, there has been a lot of interest in the subject of bullying in schools. While this is a positive development, such interest can increase fears among parents that bullying in schools is a major problem. References to bullying as a factor in some suicides has also greatly increased fears. If you are observing your child suffering anxiety and mood swings, this is deeply disturbing.

However, it is important to emphasise that the vast majority of young people at school are not bullied and do not bully others.

Question   **For what should parents watch out?**

Answer   As stated, the vast majority of students at
                 school are unaffected by bullying behaviour.
                 There is no need for parents/guardians to
                 worry unduly. However, the following signs/
                 symptoms may suggest that a student is
                 being bullied:

- a student who has been happy at school
  suddenly losing interest and enthusiasm
  for school – this may be reflected in
  deterioration in school performance;

- anxiety about travelling to and from school
  – requesting parents to drive or collect
  them;

- unwillingness to attend school – worrying
  about the route to school;

- damage to bicycles or personal property,
  for example clothes, books, or loss of
  same;

- a student returning from school in bad
  humour but reluctant to say why;

- unexplained changes of mood, which often
  occur before the restart of school – for
  example at the end of the weekend or the
  end of holidays;

- frequent minor illnesses – especially
  headaches and stomach-aches, difficulty
  in sleeping, not eating – these often
  accompany the mood changes mentioned
  above;

- an increase in requests for money;

- unexplained cuts and bruises;

- recurrent nightmares;

- bed-wetting (in the case of younger children).

These signs do not necessarily mean that a pupil is being bullied. However, if repeated, or occurring in combination, these signs do need investigation.

Question   **Why is it important to keep a written record of bullying incidents?**

Answer   A written record of incidents should be kept, with date, time, people involved and brief details. If incidents are not recorded, it can lead to confusion about when and where the incident(s) happened and how many people were involved. This concrete information also gives the school the opportunity to investigate and observe.

Question   **How can you support a child being bullied?**

Answer   It is not possible to provide total protection from bullying but you can support your child and equip them with some simple coping strategies.

• Listen in a supportive way.

• Gently establish that this is a problem bullying case and not a once-off, everyday schoolyard run-in.

• Reassure your child that the problem lies with the bully and not with them. Your child has no reason to feel foolish or guilty.

• Build up your child's self-esteem by providing plenty of positive feedback about their appearance, personality and ability.

• Try to find a rewarding outlet for their abilities through extra-curricular activities.

• Role-play the bullying situation with your child and see how they respond. Encourage them to lift their head, make eye contact and speak loudly and clearly.

• When your child is bullied in school, tell them to protest loudly: "Get away and leave me alone!" This attracts the attention of those in authority.

• Advise the child to imagine a wall around them – the bully's taunts are like arrows that fall to ground. If they can learn to keep out the negativity, they will not be so weakened by the attacks.

• Never advise retaliation, especially

physical. It gives the bully an excuse to continue their behaviour and describe it as self-defence.

Question   **What is the best way to make contact with the school?**

Answer   The best way to make contact with the school about bullying is by telephone or by letter. With the exception of very young children, going in person can put pressure on a pupil: they may be afraid of being called a "rat" or of what their classmates will think. On the phone or by letter, an appointment can be made to speak to the appropriate person.

Question   **What if the school is unsupportive?**

Answer   If the school is unwilling to act or has no
                formal procedure in place, contact the Board
                of Management and seek advice from the
                Parents' Association, if there is one.

Question **What if the bullying occurs outside the school?**

Answer If the bullying is taking place outside school property, you may involve the Gardaí. Juvenile Liaison Officers and Community Guards are very supportive in these cases and their presence at danger spots can make a difference.

Question   **What might indicate that your child is bullying?**

Answer   There are three things that could be pointers here:

1. Are they excessively aggressive with brothers and sisters?

2. How do they treat you as a parent?

3. Are they cruel to animals? (It has been established that people who are cruel to animals are quite often involved in bullying. This ties in with the fact that people who bully are often lacking in empathy. They tend not to see the world from the other person's per-spective and are therefore immune to the suffering their behaviour causes.)

Question **What would you do if your child were bullying?**

Answer Sometimes, a parent may have the unpleasant experience of being informed by the school that their child has been involved in bullying. It is difficult for any parent to accept that their child has behaved inappropriately but it is necessary to get over the shock and not to personalise the news and see it as an implied criticism of you as a parent. While some parents will work with the school to help the child to develop positive behaviour, it is usually the case that parents receiving this kind of news tend to deny the claims or even blame others. Over the years, I have learned that when you deal with the parents of a young person who is bullying, you may be dealing with someone who models bullying behaviour.

The first thing to do is to try to find out why the child is bullying. Sometimes, they may not have worked out the reason at a conscious level. With younger children, it may be that they are spoilt – perhaps they have not yet learned that they cannot always get their own way. This can cause difficulties at the start of primary school or even in playschool. However, we must be careful with the use of terms such as "bully" and "victim". These can be dangerous labels and, at the age of five or six, it is usually inaccurate to talk about children bullying. This is not to condone anti-social behaviour, but to suggest that, at this young age, it may be due to a lack of social skills rather than a deliberate intention to bully another child. Once a child reaches the age of reason, it may well be accurate to describe the behaviour as bullying. It could be a case of jealousy or insecurity. Some children become temporary bullies after a major event, such as the birth of a baby or the separation or divorce of parents.

The second thing to do is to help the child to replace the negative behaviour with something positive. It can help to get them involved in more activities both in and out of school. Create opportunities where they can display a sense of responsibility. Encourage and praise effort, not just achievement. If this approach fails to bring results, it may be necessary to look at withdrawal of privileges or use of sanctions.

Question **How can students help to create a positive atmosphere in school?**

Answer Students can help create a positive atmosphere by being involved in peer-support programmes (such as the mentor system, described in the next section); taking part in student councils; being part of events such as "friendship weeks"; and taking an active part in drawing up a code of behaviour for their class, maybe during their Social, Personal and Health Education class.

Question   **What is a peer-support/mentor programme?**

Answer   Research into bullying behaviour indicates that many pupils who are being bullied find it impossible to tell anyone about it. A peer-support programme involves older and younger pupils in the school. The older pupils act as a support to the younger ones and provide a line of communication between the teaching staff and pupils. Third Year/Transition Year students apply each year for the position in writing saying why they are applying. Selection of the mentors may be on the basis of the written application alone or may, in addition, use an interview.

Depending on the school, throughout the year the older pupils may be involved in:

- organising sports/social events (e.g. soccer tournaments, outings, competitions, table quizzes, for the younger pupils);

- supervision of the locker area at break time each morning;

- regular meetings with First Year students;

- informal contact with First Year students.

The main objectives of peer-support programmes are:

1. to create an atmosphere of friendship and trust that can ease the transition from primary to secondary school;

2. to make it easier for younger pupils to speak about difficulties they may be experiencing;

3. to promote a more positive atmosphere among the older pupils taking part and thereby help to reduce negative behaviour within their group.

Students participating in a programme such as this need training in listening skills, boundaries and use of appropriate language. It is essential that all students taking part in a programme such as this have guidelines, to ensure their protection. Ideally, they should have a major input into devising those guidelines, which would constitute a major part of the training time. A set of sample guidelines is shown below.

Guidelines for Mentors

We should:

- treat First Year students and our own group members with respect;

- be there to listen;

- be friendly;

- give information not advice;

- approach one of the adults involved in the programme in the event of a serious matter arising, for example guidance counsellor, First Year form tutors, year head, chaplain;

- treat people equally;

- act as positive role models;

- use appropriate language;

- be ourselves.

We should not:

- promise confidentiality (if the individual or somebody else is in danger, we must refer the matter on);

- make empty promises to First Year students;

- patronise;

- allow First Years to become dependent on us;

- become physically involved in conflict;

- abuse our position;

- approach a teacher about a class matter on behalf of a First Year student.

The differences that a peer-support/mentor programme can make to school include:

- allowing students from First and Fifth Year to interact in a very positive way;

- creating a positive atmosphere where people have support;

- giving younger pupils the opportunity to settle into the school;

- giving older pupils a sense of responsibility.

Question   **What is a Friendship Week?**

Answer   The idea of Friendship Week is to focus on positive rather than negative behaviour. In the past, such weeks were often referred to as "Anti-bullying" weeks, but there is a realisation now that a positive title is more likely to produce the desired outcome. Pupils can be invited to produce posters, paintings and poems on the subject of positive behaviour. These are then displayed prominently around the school.

Question   **How can drama be used to increase awareness of bullying?**

Answer   "Drama allows for the expression of feelings and emotions and ... distances the spectators from the painful reality. It can give them the confidence to discuss aspects of an issue in an impersonal, non-threatening way."[27] A greater awareness of the negative effects of bullying behaviour can be developed using this medium. "Role-playing is a further aspect of drama that teachers may use to raise awareness of bullying/indiscipline. Like drama, it has the advantage of being non-judgemental. Pupils also tend to be relaxed with it because it is a medium used to address many issues, not just bullying."[28]

The teacher facilitating role-play should be aware of the danger of creating a situation that may increase a pupil's vulnerability or reinforce bullying. Role-play is best used with a group where the teacher is familiar with the personalities involved and the dynamic within the group.

Question **What kind of guidelines could a school make available to students to help them deal with bullying?**

Answer It is important to provide written guidelines in accessible language. This creates an atmosphere of openness and emphasises that, in this school, bullying is not tolerated.

Bullying Behaviour: Guidelines for Students

Bullying is:

- negative behaviour that intimidates someone, mentally or physically;

- when a person is intentionally placed in an uncomfortable situation by another person/persons;

- continuous psychological, physical or personal intimidation;

- intentionally hurting someone.

Examples:

- physical aggression;

- damage or misplacement of another's work or property;

- extortion;

- intimidation, abusive phone calls or text messages;

- deliberate exclusion or isolation;

- slagging;

- name-calling;

- unwelcome comments;
- hitting;
- throwing items at another person;
- spreading rumours.

The excuse that any of these behaviours is "only messing" is not acceptable.

It is important to remember:

- you cannot see inside somebody else's head;
- each person has a right to be who and what they are;
- all students are entitled to an education free from fear and intimidation;
- respect should be shown to all persons at all times;
- bullies look for an excuse for what they do; they try to justify their actions by saying it is a person's fault for being different. If there is no real difference, then they will invent one.

What should you do if you are being bullied?
Do not keep it to yourself. Talk to someone you can trust – friend, brother or sister, your parents, a teacher, a member of the non-teaching staff. They are all there to help.

Remember

- It is they who are wrong, not you! There is nothing wrong in asking for help.

- Try to be assertive.

- Do not let them see that you are upset; keep your head and shoulders up; do not look down.

- Do not retaliate physically – you might end up being accused of bullying somebody yourself.

- Tell the truth about what has happened; do not exaggerate.

- Do not believe the lies that the bullies tell about you.

- Do not hide what is happening from the adults you trust.

- If you know somebody is being bullied, talk about it. This is not "ratting" – it is behaving responsibly.

- Work at developing your friendships. Do not allow yourself to become isolated. Get involved in activities in the school.

Endnotes

1. Department of Education (An Roinn Oideachais) (1993) *Guidelines on Countering Bullying Behaviour in Primary and Post-Primary Schools*, Dublin: The Stationery Office, p. 2.
2. Brendan Byrne (1994) *Bullying: A Community Approach*, Dublin: The Columba Press, p. 46.
3. Ibid., p. 12.
4. A.M. O'Moore, C. Kirkham and M. Smith. (1997) "Nation-wide Study of Bullying in Schools" *Irish Journal of Psychology*, Vol. 18, pp. 141–69.
5. M. Murray and C. Keane (1998) *The ABC of Bullying*, Dublin: Mercier Press.
6. Brendan Byrne (1992) "Bullies and Victims in a School Setting with Reference to Some Schools" *Irish Journal of Psychology*, Vol. 15, pp. 574–86.
7. I. Whitney and P.K. Smith (1993) "A Survey of the Nature and Extent of Bullying in Junior/Middle and Secondary Schools" *Education Research*, Vol. 35, pp. 3–25.
8. D. Olweus (1991) "Bully/Victim Problems among School Children: Basic Facts and Effects of a School-Based Intervention Program" in K. Rubin and D. Pepler (eds) *The Development and Treatment of Childhood Aggression*, Hillside, N.J.: Erbaum.
9. K. Rigby and P.T. Slee (1991) "Bullying among Australian School Children: Reported Behaviour and Attitudes towards Victims" *Journal of Social Psychology*, Vol. 131, pp. 615–27.
10. Department of Education, (An Roinn Oideachais) (1993). *Guidelines on Countering Bullying in Primary and Post-Primary Schools*, p. 1.
11. Ibid.
12. Ibid., p. 8.
13. Ibid., p. 9.
14. Ibid., p. 11.
15. Ibid., p. 13.
16. Ibid., p. 14.
17. Ibid., p. 13.
18. Ibid., p. 15.
19. Ibid., p. 18.
20. Ibid., p. 1.
21. Brendan Byrne (1994) *Bullying: A Community Approach*, p. 67.
22. T. Bliss and J. Tetley (1993) *Circle Time*, Bristol: Lucky Duck Publishing.

23. The answer to this question formed part of Dr Brendan Byrne's (2000) "Understanding the Needs of the Bullied Child and the Bully". Supplement in the *Guidance Counsellor's Handbook*, National Centre for Guidance in Education.
24. L. Costigan (1998) *Bullying and Harassment in the Workplace*, Dublin: The Columba Press, p. 20.
25. Ibid., p. 88.
26. Department of Education (An Roinn Oideachais) (1993) *Guidelines on Countering Bullying in Primary and Post-Primary Schools*, p. 4.
27. Brendan Byrne (1994) *Bullying: A Community Approach*, p.71.
28. Ibid., p.73.

Appendix

REFLECTIONS

REFLECTIONS

Based on Cicero's principle that "a life without reflection is a life not worth living", Sr Kathleen Maguire and I invite the participants of our courses and seminars on Confronting Bullying to spend a little time in silent reflection before each session. This affords the participants an opportunity to recall the past with its bad memories of bullying instances. The recall is done during the reflections in the calm moments of the present. In this way, the participants can get in touch with their inner selves and call on the transcendent powers that reach beyond their own horizons to help them. The reflective experience can help the participants to discover their inner strengths and a capacity to address their problem of bullying in the future and to heal the psychological wounds inflicted by their tormentors.

I do not suggest that these reflections will be suitable for all the readers of this book. However, participants at our courses have indicated in their written evaluations that they have found these reflections to be very helpful, illuminating and therapeutic. For that reason, I would suggest to those readers who are victims that they might enter a quiet space, light some candles, play soft, reflective music and use the following reflections to help them in their search for inner peace and tranquillity.

Rev. Dr Tony Byrne CSSp

MY RIGHTS

The bully cannot take away

- **My right to work with dignity**
- **My right to be respected**
- **My right to have peace**
- **My right to freedom from ridicule**
- **My right to my honour**
- **My right to be Me**

Silent reflection

Spend some time slowly repeating the above phrases in your mind.

Say this prayer very slowly and reflectively

Lord, help me to be assertive and to defend my dignity, which you gave to me when you made me in your image and likeness. Help me to believe in myself as a person of worth and ability.

CONFRONTING THE BULLY

I will not submit to the bully and I will not accept

- **The bully's constant criticism and scorn**
- **The bully calling me a fool and incompetent**
- **The bully isolating me and persecuting me**
- **The bully degrading me and oppressing me**
- **The bully shouting at me**
- **The bully tormenting me**

Silent reflection

Spend some time slowly repeating the above phrases in your mind.

Say this prayer very slowly and reflectively

Lord, liberate me from the fear of the bully who is tormenting me. Give me courage to confront this bully and help me to do it without hate or anger. Give me inner strength to be assertive so that I will be freed from all that destroys my happiness and peace.

I DO NOT WANT TO ACCEPT BULLYING IN MY HOME

I will not allow myself to be bullied any more. I do not have to suffer from

- **The bully leaving me without money for the home**
- **The bully restricting my social contacts**
- **The bully calling me dumb and stupid**
- **The bully ridiculing me and my parents**
- **The bully controlling my life and excluding me**
- **The bully dictating to me**

Silent reflection

Spend some time slowly repeating the above phrases in your mind.

Say this prayer very slowly and reflectively

Lord, liberate me from the fear of the bully in my home who is tormenting me. Give me the courage to confront the bully and help me to enjoy peace, harmony and happiness in my home.

Defending My Child Who Is Bullied

I will defend my child who is bullied with all my heart and mind and strength

- **From those who bully my child**
- **From teasing and taunting**
- **From fear and self-blame**
- **From feelings of inferiority and intimidation**
- **From feelings of worthlessness and powerlessness**
- **From the pain of being mocked and tormented**

Silent reflection

Spend some time slowly repeating the above phrases in your mind.

Say this prayer slowly and reflectively

Lord, lover of children, full of compassion and mercy, come to my aid and help me to know what I should do to free my child from bullies. Put your healing hands on my child so that the painful effects of bullying may be removed.

DURING BAD TIMES LET ME REMEMBER

- **That the snow always melts**
- **That dawn comes after darkness**
- **That the rainbow may be near at hand**
- **That the hard times will become a distant past**
- **That after Good Friday comes Easter Sunday**

Silent reflection

Spend some time slowly repeating the above phrases in your mind

Say this prayer very slowly and reflectively

Lord, free me from the darkness of today. Help me to experience the light of tomorrow. Let me remember that you are there for me with your strength, love and compassion.

CONVERSION OF BULLIES

Bullies need help because they

- **Feel inferior and threatened**

- **Feel a need to control others**

- **Have a poor self-image**

- **Are not happy people**

Silent reflection

Spend some time slowly repeating the above phrases in your mind.

Say this prayer very slowly and reflectively

Lord, help the bully to change. Convert their hearts of aggression and hate into hearts of love and service for others, especially the weak and powerless.

RECOMMENDED READING

Adams, Andrea with Neil Crawford (1992) *Bullying at Work*, London: Virago Press.

Anti-Bullying, Research and Resource Centre (1998) *Workplace Bullying: Key Facts*, Dublin Education Department, Trinity College.

Breckman, Risa S. and Adelman, Ronald D. (1998) *Strategies for Helping Victims of Elder Mistreatment*, London: Sage Publications.

Byrne, Brendan (1993) *Coping with Bullying in Schools,* Dublin: The Columba Press.

Byrne, Brendan (1994) *Bullying: A Community Approach,* Dublin:The Columba Press.

Byrne, Brendan (2000) "Understanding the Needs of the Bullied Child and the Bully", Supplement in *The Guidance Counsellor's Handbook*, National Centre for Guidance in Education.

Byrne, Tony (1992) *How to Evaluate*, Ndola, Zambia: Mission Press.

Byrne, Tony (1983) *Integral Development*, Ndola, Zambia: Mission Press.

Byrne, Tony (1998) *Working for Justice and Peace*, Ndola, Zambia: Mission Press.

Clayton, Peter (2003) *Body Language at Work*, London: Petersen Publishing Ltd.

Costigan, Lucy (1998) *Bullying and Harassment in the Workplace*, Dublin: The Columba Press.

Department of Education (An Roinn Oideachais) (1993) *Guidelines on Countering Bullying Behaviour in Schools*, Dublin: The Stationery Office.

Eardly, John (2002) *Bullying and Stress in the Workplace*, Dublin: First Law Ltd.

Elliott, Michele (1998) *Bullying: Wise Guides*, London: Hodder Children's Books.

Field, Tim (1996) *Bullying in Sight,* Oxfordshire: Success Unlimited.

Fitzgerald, David (1999) *Bullying in our Schools,* Dublin: Blackhall Publishing.

Fitzgerald, David (1999) *Parents and the Bullying Problem,* Dublin: Blackhall Publishing.

Freire, Paulo and Antonio Faundez (1989) *Learning to Question,* New York: The Continuum Publishing Company.

Garratt, Daren, Roche, Jeremy and Tucker, Stanley (2002) *Changing Experiences of Youth,* London: Sage Publications.

Goddard, Trisha (2003) *The Family Survival Guide,* London: Vermillion.

Graves, David (2002) *Fighting Back: Overcoming Bullying in the Workplace,* London: The McGraw-Hill Companies.

Higgs, Robert (2002) *What have I ever done to you?* Cambridge, UK: Pegasus.

Keane, Colm (1994) *Nervous Breakdown,* Dublin: RTE and Mercier Press.

Kelly, Kate (2003) *The Baffled Parents' Guide to Stopping Bad Behaviour,* London: Contemporary Books.

Kelly, Lorraine (2003) *Real Life Solutions,* London: Century Random House Group Ltd.

Lawson, Sarah (1994) *Helping Children Cope with Bullying,* London: Sheldon Press.

McCarthy, Paul, Sheehan, Michael and Wilkie, William (1996) *Bullying from Backyard to Boardroom,* Queensland, Australia: Millennium Books.

Marr, Neil and Frield, Tim (2001) *Bullycide: Death at Playtime,* Oxfordshire: Success Unlimited.

Murray, Marie and Keane, C. (1998) *The ABC of Bullying,* Dublin: Mercier Press.

North Eastern Health Board (2002) *The Cool School Programme Series,* Drogheda, Co. Louth, Ireland: North Eastern Health Board.

O'Donnell, Vivette (1998) *The Campaign against Bullying,* Dublin: Attic Press.

Ó Laighléis, Ré (1996) *Ecstasy,* Dublin: Poolbeg Press.

Olweus, D. (1993) *Bullying at School: What we Know and What we Can Do,* Oxford: Blackwell.

Report of the Task Force on the Prevention of Workplace Bullying (2001): First National Survey on Workplace Bullying conducted by ESRI.

Rigby, K. (1996) *Bullying in Schools – and what to do about it*, Melbourne: ACER.

Scanzoni, John (2002) *Designing Families*, London: Sage Publications Ltd.

Smith, P.K., Morita, Y., Junger-Tas, J., Olweus, D., Catalano, R. and Slee, P. (eds) (1999) *The Nature of School Bullying: A Cross-National Perspective*, London: Routledge.

Sullivan, Karen (2003) *How to say 'No' and mean it*, London: Thorsons, Harper Collins Publishers.

Tattum, Delwyn P. and Lane, David A. (1994) *Bullying in Schools*, Stoke-on-Trent, UK: Trentham Books Ltd.

Thompson, Davis, Arose, Terry and Sharp, Sonia (2002) *Effective Strategies for Long-Term Improvement*, London: Routledge Falmer.

INDEX